Adventures in Numberland

a story of numbers in
life and in business

Paul Georgiou

Published by
Panarc International 2016

Copyright © Paul Georgiou, 2016

First Edition

The author asserts the moral right
under the Copyright, Designs and Patents Act 1988
to be identified as the author of this work.

All rights reserved. No part of this publication may be
reproduced, stored in a retrieval system or transmitted, in any
form or by any means without the prior consent of the author,
nor be otherwise circulated in any form of binding or cover
other than that in which it is published and without a similar
condition being imposed on the subsequent purchaser.

www.panarcpublishing.com
Panarc International Ltd
www.panarc.com

ISBN: 978-0-9954637-5-2
Epub: 978-0-9954637-6-9
Kindle: 978-0-9954637-7-6

Cover design and typesetting by
Chandler Book Design

Printed in the United Kingdom
by Ingram Sparks

1

Once upon a time there was a girl called Stephanie, living in a forest in the county of Numberland in the far north of England.

Before we go any further, I need to clarify three points.

Although the girl's name was Stephanie, she preferred to be called Piff, so that is what I shall call her from this point on. Why she preferred Piff, you may wonder, but it must remain a secret. (On the other hand, by the end of the story you will discover why all numbers are interesting and, in particular, why the number 999 came to be of such importance in Numberland and, indeed, elsewhere.)

Secondly, when I say Piff lived in the forest, I don't mean she survived unprotected, roughing it under the trees on the forest's ferny floor. No, she had a home, the cottage of her father, Jack, the woodcutter.

Thirdly, she lived in the county of Numberland. That's Numberland, not Northumberland. Numberland was a small English county sandwiched between Northumberland, to the north-east; Scotland to the north-west and Cumberland to the south. Sadly, Numberland no longer exists, having been abolished in some boundary changes in the second half of the last century.

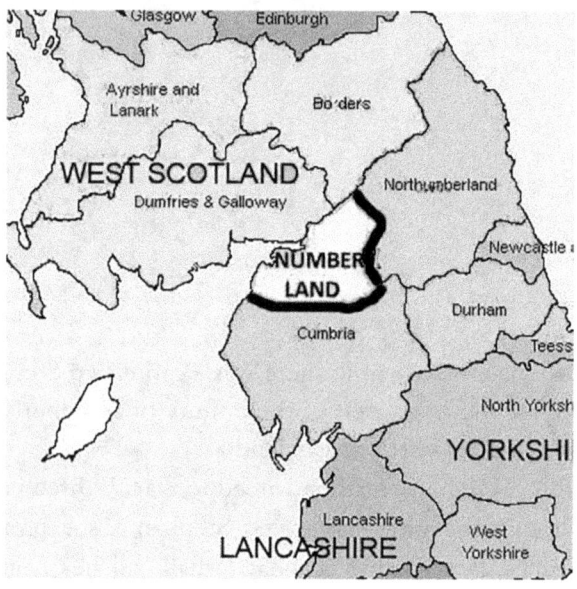

Of course you would like me to get on with the narrative but it is always important to be clear about everything if you're telling a story.

2

So Piff lived in the cottage in the forest with her father, Jack, and her stepmother, Jill.

Jack was a woodcutter. He made a living by cutting wood in the forest and selling it to the villagers who dwelt in the nearby village.

I should explain that Jack, who was a very thin person, was hard-working but not ambitious and lacked drive. Jill, on the other hand, was very fat and lazy. When they were courting, they had both sustained some serious head injuries whilst engaged in a water collecting exercise which, if we're feeling generous, could explain their total lack of initiative. Why on earth they were climbing a hill when wells tend to be low down, rather than high up, remains a mystery to this day.

Anyway, the point is that the family was poor and getting poorer, as a result of a decline in the price of wood and an increase in rent imposed by the cruel and rapacious Prince Baltigral, the owner of the cottage and almost everything else in Numberland.

3

One day, Jill sat Jack down and demanded to know what her husband planned to do about their financial situation. More precisely she wanted to discuss the allocation of sausages.

Like everyone in Numberland, the family lived on a diet of bread and Numberland sausages. When times were good, dinner consisted of a thick slice of bread and a varying number of large Numberland sausages, washed down with the cheap but nutritious befangle juice. In the good times, Jack and Jill had three sausages; Piff had two. When the price of wood fell and times had got harder, Jack had dropped his quota to two; Piff to one. Jill insisted her body would cease to function if she had less than three. Further cuts in the sausage ration became necessary, so Jack said he would drop down to one. Jill, who was a bit of a glutton, continued to insist on her quota of three. While they could afford five sausages, all was well, although obviously Jack and Piff were hungry most of the time.

Then the day came when they could afford only four sausages a day. It looked very much as though Jill would have to give up one of her sausages. This prospect did not please Jill and, since it was Piff who had said it was obvious she must relinquish a sausage, Jill's anger was focused on Piff.

"I don't see why you and Piff can't share a sausage," Jill had suggested to her husband.

"That's not possible, my dear," Jack had objected. "I am already so weak I find it hard to cut the wood. If I can't cut the wood, there will be no sausages."

"In that case," Jill replied, "if your daughter's so keen you should have a whole sausage, perhaps she should give you hers."

Jack objected. "That would mean Piff would have to live on bread alone."

"Or she could leave home, get a job and feed herself," snapped Jill.

Now Jack loved his daughter but it was true that, from the time he had remarried following the death of Piff's mother, there had been a good deal of tension in the cottage, and not just about the allocation of sausages. Jill and Piff didn't get on. Truth to tell, Jill was jealous of her beautiful stepdaughter who had been blessed with light auburn hair, blue/grey eyes, a lovely face and a perfect complexion.

"She's a little young to set out on her own," Jack objected.

"She's 14 years old," Jill replied sharply. "When I was her age, I'd already been befangle mangling for three years."

In passing I should tell you that the befangle was a fruit, native to Numberland, which Numberlanders put through a befangle mangle to extract the vitamin-laden juice. There was even a popular Numberland befangling song:

When, from trees, befangles dangle
and you've coin enough to jangle,
> *whether you be blest or cursed,*
> *be the first to quench your thirst*
and see the knot of life untangle.

'Tis so easy, all you do
is take the fruit, plump, round and true
> *and, whether you be cursed or blest,*
turn the handle of your mangle
through the perfect squelching angle;
> *wind and grind and do your best*
> *or, failing best, pray do your worst,*
to crush to mush the fruit befangle.

Never worry, what's the use?
Life's a gift, there no excuse.
> *Do not argue, carp or wrangle,*
> *grab each bonus you can wangle.*
Always wear your tunic loose.
> *In these words you are well versed:*
"Take the cup of golden juice
> *and drink befangle till you burst".*

The fruit was plentiful and befangle juice was therefore cheap. You could buy a flagon of befangle juice for not much more than half the cost of a single Numberland sausage.

Anyway, back to the story. Jack was uneasy about Jill's suggestion that Piff should leave home and fend for herself but Jill was undeterred; she would talk to Piff and see what she said.

4

That afternoon, while Jack was out cutting wood, Jill cornered Piff and told her that she and Jack had been discussing the future.

"Given the circumstances, your father and I have agreed it would be best if you left home," said Jill.

"Is that what Dad wants?" Piff had asked, quite shocked.

"I just told you that's what we agreed," said Jill.

"And when am I supposed to go?" asked Piff, now seriously worried as well as shocked.

"Now's as good a time as any," said Jill.

"But I haven't got any money," said Piff.

"What a surprise!" snapped Jill. "Could that be because you don't work? You live here in our house eating our sausages. Befangle fruit may grow on trees but money doesn't. It's time you took some responsibility for yourself rather than leeching off me and your father."

Now it has to be said that Piff had a bit of a temper and a great deal of pride. She wasn't going to be put down by her stepmother.

"Very well," said Piff. "I will go but if there's anyone leeching around here, it's you. I help Dad with wood gathering, clean the house and cook the sausages. What do you do? I think Dad was mad to marry you. You don't love him. You're a mean, greedy person. If you loved him, you'd give him one of your sausages."

"And if he didn't love me," said Jill, "he would take it. So there."

Piff didn't really understand the point Jill was making, but she was too upset to continue the exchange of views.

"I'll just collect my belongings and then I'll be on my way," said Piff.

"What belongings?" enquired Jill. "There's nothing here that belongs to you."

"I'll take the abacus that Dad gave me last Christmas," said Piff defiantly. "That's mine because it was a present."

"Take the useless thing," said Jill, eager to be rid of her stepdaughter before Jack returned.

"It's not useless," said Piff, just to have the last word.

Of course, it was useless but she wouldn't admit it. Last December, before the bottom had dropped out of the firewood market, her father had found the abacus mixed up with some second-hand shoes in a cart boot sale, and bought it for her. He had liked the beads on the wires, thinking it was a toy.

5

It was late afternoon when Piff set off into the forest. It would take a couple of hours on foot to reach the nearest village and she was not entirely sure of the way. When, in the past, she had travelled through the forest with her father to sell their firewood, they had taken the horse and cart. Her father had driven and Piff had not paid much attention to the route. To the untutored eye, one pathway through the trees looked much the same as any other.

The sun was sinking low in the sky. Piff had two worries; first that, even if she was on the right path, she might not reach the village before darkness; secondly, that she was lost and might have to wander the forest for days, weeks, years or, possibly, for ever.

She found a tree stump, sat down with her only possession held tightly in her hand, and began to cry. A large tear trickled down her cheek and then dropped on to one of the beads on the top row of the abacus.

6

"Why so glum?" enquired a high-pitched, melodious voice, as clear as a bell.

Piff almost fell off the tree stump. "Who said that?" she managed to say.

"There's only you and me here, apart from the innumerable but inarticulate squirrels, rabbits, birds and spiders," said the voice. "So, if it wasn't you, it must have been me."

Piff looked everywhere. There was no one.

"Up here," said the voice. There, sitting on the low branch of a nearby tree was a very beautiful fairy, about 18 inches (or 46 centimetres) long. She had soft blonde hair, clear blue eyes, a graceful form and gossamer wings.

"Wow!" said Piff, who had stopped sobbing. Of course Piff had heard of fairies. The country folk of Numberland were always telling tales of fairies, good and bad, and witches and wizards, and all manner of elfin types – but Piff had never seen any of them before.

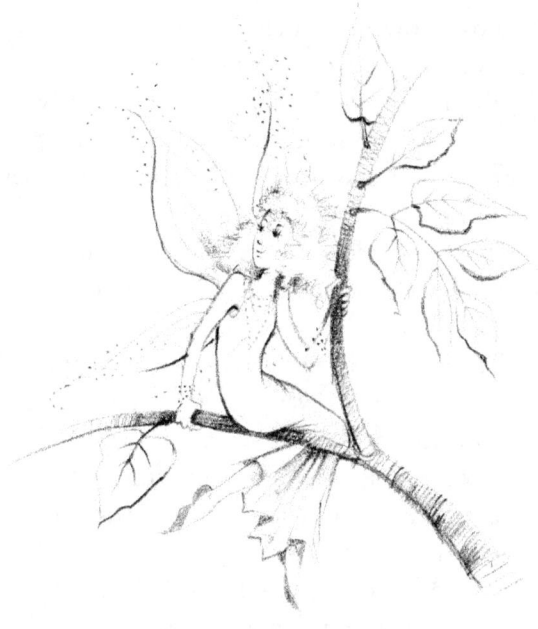

"That's an odd name for a humanite," the fairy laughed, assuming that Piff had just introduced herself. "Well, Wow, my name is Numberlina, and I am one of a band of elite fairies known as the Numerati."

"My name's not Wow," said Piff. "I was surprised to see you so I exclaimed 'Wow!'. My name is Piff and I am the woodcutter's daughter."

"The woodcutter's daughter, I see," said Numberlina. "And what are you doing, wandering alone in the forest, far away from your home, when the sun is setting?"

Piff began to sob again.

"Lesson one," said Numberlina. "Crying won't float your boat."

"What does that mean?" asked Piff. "I don't have a boat."

"Of course you don't," Numberlina agreed. "But, if you had a boat, however much you cried, there would be insufficient water to get your boat off the ground. We fairies are much given to proverbs and sayings which we use to record the wisdom of our people. I was just telling you that crying is pretty pointless. It doesn't make things better, so it's a waste of time."

"You're not very sympathetic," Piff complained.

"Why should I be sympathetic? I don't know why you're crying."

So Piff told Numberlina what had happened. She explained that her family was very poor because of a drop in the price of firewood, that her father Jack couldn't earn enough to feed them, that her stepmother Jill demanded three sausages a day, come what may, and that she, Piff, had been thrown out of her home.

"Shucks, that sucks," observed Numberlina. "Your stepmother doesn't sound like a very nice person. But not to fret. Your luck is about to change."

"Shucks, that sucks," Piff repeated. "What does that mean?"

You should know that country folk in Numberland spoke only plain English, using a strictly limited and straightforward vocabulary. They were unfamiliar with colloquialisms.

"'Shucks' is an expression of resignation and surprise," Numberlina explained. "'Sucks' indicates that something is bad. The expression is popular with fairy folk because it rhymes. We like rhymes."

Piff accepted the explanation.

"Well aren't you going to ask me?" Numberlina seemed disappointed.

"Ask you what?"

"I just told you that your luck was about to change,"

Numberlina said in a voice that hinted patience was not her strongest suit.

"So what?" said Piff. "It's nice of you to be encouraging I suppose, but it doesn't really help. I'm still lost in the forest, with nowhere to go, nothing to eat and no place safe to sleep."

"I wasn't trying to be encouraging, I was offering to help," said Numberlina. She opened her wings, and elegantly glided down to Piff's tree stump. "Lift and shift," she said. "There's room for both of us."

"How can you help?" asked Piff. "I need somewhere to shelter. Even if you've got a home, I doubt if I'd fit into to it."

"Buck up, you shmuck!" said Numberlina. "I'm talking the big picture."

"You have a very funny way with words," said Piff.

Numberlina ignored Piff's comment. "I am going to grant you one wish."

"Really?" said Piff. Numberlina now had Piff's full attention. Like most forest children, Piff had been brought up on stories of meetings with fairy folk who offered to grant a person one or more wishes. When her mother had been alive, most evenings she had told Piff such stories at bedtime. An important feature of all such stories was that you had to be careful in choosing your wish because, for some obscure reason, fairy folk took delight in tricking humans. If, for example, you wished to be rich all the days of your life, they would give you a load of money, closely followed by bubonic plague, so you were rich for a just a few days before you died.

"I'd like to have a long, happy and successful life," said Piff after a few moments' thought. She was rather pleased with herself.

"Just a couple of problems there," said Numberlina. "First, I said I would grant you one wish. That is three wishes.

We fairies tend to respond badly to greed. Secondly, you misunderstood. I'm going to grant you one wish but I decide what the wish is."

"Well, I don't want to seem ungrateful," said Piff, "but you're not granting me a wish if I can't choose which wish to wish."

"You humanites," said Numberlina, now quite irritated. "You seem to think that we fairies can just grant wishes willy-nilly. You don't understand, we all have our specialities. You wouldn't ask a bricklayer to do embroidery, or a moral philosopher to run a crime syndicate."

Piff thought of arguing the first point. A bricklayer might well take up embroidery for relaxation. But she decided against it because, regarding the second point, she didn't know what a moral philosopher or a crime syndicate was. So she let it go.

"Well then, what's your speciality?" Piff asked, in a mildly interested tone.

"Numbers," Numberlina replied. "I am Numberlina, a fairy of the Numerati. The clue's in the name. I have a cousin called Agravarable; he's into farming; a sister Grammaria, who works with words and a rich uncle called Spondulox. I myself do numbers."

"Really," said Piff, the mild interest entirely excised from her voice.

"Well, don't you want to know how I'm going to help you?" asked Numberlina, now hurt by Piff's attitude.

"Frankly," said Piff, "I don't think you can help me at all, unless you can tell me where the nearest village is and how to get there as quickly as possible. As for numbers, they've never been of much interest to me. I don't even like mathematics."

"You don't like mathematics?" exclaimed Numberlina, as though Piff had just said she didn't like chocolate cake. "Then why are you carrying an abacus? You may think you don't like maths but you do or, if you don't, you will. Numbers will give you food and shelter; numbers will help you to accumulate money; numbers can make you powerful. You said you wanted a long, happy and successful life. Numbers will give you the best hope of fulfilling that wish."

Piff shrugged. Obviously Numberlina was an enthusiast.

"Come with me," said Numberlina. "There's something I want to show you."

7

Numberlina moved through the trees. She flew slowly so that Piff could easily keep pace with her, and as she flew, she cast a warm, bright light on the ground so that Piff could avoid any fallen branches or rabbit holes.

After a few minutes, Piff saw a bright orange glow in the distance. As she drew closer she could see the glow was a large dome of light, entirely encasing a wide circular clearing in the forest.

"This is my home," said Numberlina proudly, hovering at Piff's eye height. "It's always pleasantly warm and dry inside the dome and there's plenty of food and drink. I even have guest quarters, as you can see, on the far side, to accommodate the occasional visitor. Come in and make yourself comfortable."

Now Piff was cold and hungry and it was beginning to rain but Piff was no fool.

"Why are you helping me?" she asked. "And what do you want?"

Numberlina looked surprised. "Don't you trust me?" She sounded hurt.

"It's not that I don't trust you but I need to know why you are being so kind. You must want something from me."

Numberlina was charmed by Piff's frankness and replied with equal honesty. "I want three things from you. I want your company because sometimes I feel lonely. I want gold, 15% of the gold you earn through the help I give you, and thirdly," – here she hesitated, fearing this third requirement might be a deal breaker – "thirdly, I need your help in handling the Anathemath."

The first demand was not a problem. Piff also felt lonely. She had been thrown out of her home by her stepmother; she was lost, hungry and afraid. Numberlina was an odd companion but she seemed to be friendly and, since she was the only company on offer, Piff was in no position to be picky.

The second demand was also easy to accept. Piff had never seen a piece of gold in her life, much less owned one. If, by any chance, Numberlina could ever help Piff to acquire gold, then she was more than welcome to a share of it. True, Piff was a bit hazy on percentages but she knew that the whole of anything was 100%, so 15% didn't sound too much; it still left her 85%.

It was the third condition that worried Piff. "What exactly is the Anathemath and what does 'handling' mean?"

"You don't have to worry about him," said Numberlina reassuringly. "He's more a nuisance than a serious problem. My branch of the fairy family tree is concerned with getting things right. We're professionals. Whether it's words, or numbers, or farming or banking, or any other speciality, we like to make sure everything is in order and works properly. The Anathemath takes a perverse pleasure in trying to mess things up."

"I see," said Piff slowly. "So what would you expect me to do?"

"Nothing really, well very little," Numberlina replied dismissively. "If he tries to interfere, or trick you, or confuse you, I need you to stand up to him and help me put him in his place. Is that all right?"

Numberlina's demands seemed reasonable to Piff and, in any case, the warm orange dome looked so inviting and the promise of food and shelter was so appealing that she was very eager to enjoy the offered hospitality. Mind you, she had a funny feeling there might be more to dealing with the Anathemath than Numberlina was prepared to admit.

"Fair enough," said Piff.

"Fairy Nuff! You know Nuff," Numberlina exclaimed. "I assumed I was the first fairy you had met."

Piff was puzzled. She explained: "I know no Nuff. I was just saying I agree."

Now Numberlina was really puzzled. No Nuff was the black sheep of the Nuff fairy family. While most of the Nuffs were engaged in the application of herbs for medicinal purposes, No Nuff took a generally negative attitude to everything. He refused to undertake any type of work, claiming he suffered from low back pain or depression and preferring to rely on the generous fay folk welfare arrangements and free medical assistance provided by the National Elf Service.

Realising that she and Piff might be talking at cross purposes, Numberlina decided to let the matter rest. "Then let's go in," she said.

8

Piff settled down on a toadstool which Numberlina had kindly enlarged to support a human form.

"What would you like to eat?" asked Numberlina.

Now Piff had only ever eaten bread and sausages, and wild fruit, so she had no idea what to ask for. "What do you have?" she asked.

Numberlina laughed. "I know you Numberlanders. You're very fond of sausages. But why don't you try something different. I can magic up anything you like. It's a perk of being one of the fairy folk. I suggest a nice crusty steak and kidney pie."

So it was that Piff began to realise that there were other forms of food than bread and sausages. She greatly enjoyed her meal.

When they had finished eating and drinking, they settled down for a chat.

"After munching, number crunching," said Numberlina, "You will recall I promised to grant you the gift of numbers.

You didn't seem to be very keen but you will learn. The first thing you need to do is meet them. So I'm going to tell you a story."

Piff settled herself on some fairy down, made herself comfortable and was ready to listen. So Numberlina began:

> *Once upon a time, an argument began between the numbers from which all numbers are made. Why the argument started no one is sure. That is often the way with arguments. No one can remember how they start. I suspect the Anathemath had something to do with it. No matter. I'll just get on with the story.*
>
> *The even numbers 2, 4, 6 and 8, all of whom were female, decided that they were clearly superior to the odd numbers, all of whom were male.*
>
> *"We are evenly balanced," the even numbers said. "Each of us can be divided into two equal, perfectly balanced numbers. What is more, you other numbers are decidedly odd."*
>
> *The odd numbers 1, 3, 5, 7 and 9 could not dispute that they were odd but they were not ready to accept defeat.*
>
> *"Hold it right there," said One, a handsome, straight-backed and, let's face it, rather self-centred individual. "You may be perfectly balanced but most of us odd numbers are prime numbers. Prime means first in rank. We can be divided only by ourselves and me. That means we are special. In my case, I'm extra special because I can be divided only by me and*

myself. It must be obvious to you even numbers that we prime numbers are superior to you."

There was a lot of muttering. The prime numbers Three, Five and Seven were pleased by One's argument for the specialness of the odd numbers – although they couldn't help noticing that he, One, was claiming to be extra special.

Then Number Two, a clever, thoughtful girl, with brown eyes and close cropped brown hair, spoke. What she said met with a mixed response.

"I am an even number and I am also a prime number. Indeed I am the only prime number that is even," said Two. "I am therefore superior to all of you. And, since you've raised the matter, I've some bad news for One. You're not a prime number. To be a prime number you have to be greater than One. This means I, Two, am the first prime number." Here Two paused for effect. "You could say that I, Two, am number one amongst numbers. So give me some respect."

If there had been muttering before, now there was hubbub. The even numbers were pleased that Two, an even number, had put the odd numbers in their place but were not happy that she was claiming to be pre-eminent amongst even numbers. Indeed she was making a bid to be pre-eminent amongst all numbers. They were even more upset when they realised that Two's claim to pre-eminence was mainly based on being a prime number which, to some extent, supported the odd numbers claim to superiority, at least for Three, Five and Seven – Nine being the only odd number, apart from One, not a prime.

At this point, Numberlina took a breath.

"You're talking about the numbers as though they were people," Piff remarked. "That's just your way of telling the story, I assume?"

"Yes and no," said Numberlina. "Of course when you count something – apples oranges, pieces of gold – you come up with a number: 2 apples, 3 oranges, 1,000 pieces of gold. You could say that what matters when you count things, is the things you count; not the number which is merely the number of those important things that happen to be present. You could say that it's the apples, the oranges and the gold that are important. But numbers matter too. There's a big difference between one piece of gold and nine pieces of gold. And numbers, believe me, have a life of their own, quite apart from the things they can be used to count. And, in this story, which is also your story, the numbers are very much alive. They're fairly small, smaller than you but bigger than me. Some are male and some are female. And they all have their own character. Each of them has an interesting tale to tell. You need to get to know them. And when you feel comfortable in their company, I can begin to show you how they can help to make you happy, rich and powerful."

"I hope it won't get too complicated," said Piff.

Numberlina smiled. "It as simple as 1, 2, 3. Anyway, let's get back to the story. Now I don't know about you, Piff, but I love a really good argument. Not a fight to the death, you understand but a vigorous discussion in which each participant fights his corner. (That's a boxing metaphor. We fairies don't actually box, being too insubstantial and ethereal.) Anyway, that's what happened next.

> *The voice of Six, a very pretty, well-turned out young lady, with blue eyes, rose out of the hubbub. "If anyone is to be pre-eminent, it must be me. After all, I am the only perfect number amongst us."*

> *"What's so perfect about you?" asked Eight, a rather plump girl who, truth to tell, had always been a little envious of the pretty, slim Six.*

> *Six tossed her head, without putting one of her golden blonde curls out of place, and explained in a slightly*

haughty tone, "It's a technical term. I am perfect because all my divisors add up to me."

"What's a divisor?" asked Eight. Six's claim to perfection sounded like gobbledegook (not a technical Numblish term but a reference to the incoherent noise of geese or turkeys, I believe).

"Divisors," said Six, now with a more pronounced haughty tone, "are all the whole smaller numbers that can divide a bigger whole number perfectly without leaving anything over. In my case, I have three factors – 1, 2 and 3. 1 goes into 6, 6 times. 2 goes into 6, 3 times. And 3 goes into 6, twice. If the divisors of a number, excluding the number itself, add up to that number, that number is perfect. My divisors, 1, 2, 3, add up to me, 6. Thus I, Six, am the only perfect number among us and should we wish to appoint a leader, surely that leader should be me."

"Hold on," Two interrupted. "You may be the first perfect number, but, if 8 and I stand together, with me in the first position of course, we make 28, and I think you'll find 28 is the next perfect number. Its divisors are 1, 2, 4, 7 and 14. Add them up and they total 28. So, to summarise," said Two in the most irritatingly superior tone, "I am not only the first prime, the first even number, and the only even number that is a prime; I am also the major partner in the second perfect number."

"That's all very well but you, on your own, are not a perfect number," said Six dismissively, "whereas I am.

You can't be perfect if you need someone else to make you perfect."

The odd numbers were pleased to see disunity amongst the even numbers. Two and Six were now close to an exchange of personal insults. Eight joined in on the side of Two, rather flattered to be coupled with Two in making up the second perfect number 28, and more than happy to take Six down a peg or two.

"Now, now, girls," said One patronisingly. "You don't hear us odd numbers bickering amongst ourselves.

Two was irritated by One's condescending tone. Secretly, she rather fancied One but her feelings were not reciprocated. As her friend Eight had told her, the only person One loved was himself.

"We're not bickering," said Two. "We're having a serious discussion which, if you odd numbers have anything to contribute, you are welcome to join."

"I think all the discussion so far," said Seven, who was a ladies' man, a bit of a rogue and a charmer, "has been stultifyingly academic. The most important feature of any number is personality, nothing to do with maths. Take me. I'm lucky. I have a bit of magic about me. And I'm very popular with humans. There's the seven ages of man; the seven pillars of wisdom; the seven wonders of the world and," here he winked at Six, "the seven deadly sins."

"I wouldn't for a minute wish to question Seven's characterisation of his personality," said Five, a serious

and sometimes pompous individual, "but, if we're going to talk about human respect for numbers, I doubt if anyone would wish to dispute my pre-eminence."
"I might," said Seven, with a grin. "Prove your point."

"Well now, let me see," said Five. There are the five elements of the ancient Greeks (fire, water, earth, air and ether)."

"That's not much of an argument," said Four, a rather stolid and opinionated young girl, who had kept quiet so far. "I mean, ether doesn't exist so there were really only four elements."
"That's not the point," said Five. "They thought there were five elements. In any case, that was just one example. There are five elements in ancient Indian tradition (earth, fire, sky, water and air); five in Japanese philosophy; five elements in feng shui. Then there's the five wounds of Christ; and the Five Pillars of Islam. I could go on."

"And you do," said Seven provocatively.

"You're on dangerous ground," said Nine to Five. "If we're talking religious significance, I think you'll find that I am seen as the main man. After all, I symbolise completeness in Hinduism and Bahai."

"Hold on," Three interrupted. "Of all numbers, I, Three, am surely the most magical and holy." Three, a pale, good-looking young man, with soft skin and gentle eyes, was regarded by his fellow odd numbers as the male most in touch with his feminine side. "I represent the union of One and Two. And were there not, I seem to recall, three Graces in the religion of ancient Greece: Beauty, Charm and Joy? Is it not the case that all good fairy stories lean heavily on me, invariably offering three wishes, three attempts at every riddle, three choices for success or salvation? Furthermore," he added as his clincher, "I am the lynchpin of the Christian Trinity: Father, Son and Holy Spirit."

> *"Very good," said Nine. "All good arguments well presented. But I speak as the square of Three. Three times Three is Nine. If Three is blessed, then surely I, Nine, am thrice blessed."*
>
> *Two interrupted with a laugh. "Well I think you've just proved that you odd numbers can bicker with the best of us."*

Numberlina stopped her story-telling. Piff had curled up on a bed of fairy down and fallen asleep.

"Oh well," said Numberlina. "At least we've made a start."

9

The following morning, Piff awoke early. The sun was streaming into the dome. The air was warm. And Piff felt better than she had for a very long time.

"You slept well," said Numberlina.

"I feel great," said Piff. "Is there something magic here?"

"Well, since you're in a fairy dome talking to a fairy, it's a fair bet that there's magic in the air but, if you want my opinion on the cause of your well-being, I'd credit the steak and kidney pudding. That's probably the first decent meal you've had in years."

Piff laughed. "It certainly was delicious."

"You nodded off last night when I was in the middle of a story," Numberlina reminded Piff.

"Yes, I'm really sorry. I did hear most of it but I was so tired."

"Don't worry," said Numberlina. "I just wanted you to meet the numbers. Today, we will begin to see how they can help us. But first, breakfast — or, as we fairies always say in our advice to young humanites, 'Chomp before you yomp'. As you've had such a limited diet in the past, allow me to suggest what you should have. I think a glass of orange juice, followed by a bacon omelette, and toast and marmalade."

"Is that what you're having?" asked Piff.

Numberlina smiled. "I think not. We fairies don't eat. We live on the perfume of roses, on the gentle scent of honeysuckle, on the goodness in another's happy laughter. But such nutrition will not sustain a humanite. We know what humanites need. Orange juice, omelette, and toast and marmalade is an excellent breakfast for you. So I won't eat but I will keep you company."

After breakfast, Numberlina and Piff sat together. Numberlina began with a question. "You said your family was poor. Your father is a woodcutter. It tends to be a seasonal job but, even in the summer, there's some demand for wood and, in the winter, you can sell it at a premium. So why are you poor?"

"What's a premium?" asked Piff. "We only ever sell it in the markets in the villages."

"A premium is not a place. It's a higher price which is justified by a higher than usual demand. When something is scarce, people will pay more for it."

Piff immediately understood the point Numberlina was making and started to wonder why her father always sold his sacks of firewood at the same price throughout the year.

"I'm not sure why we are so poor," Piff tried to answer Numberlina's question. "My father works hard. I guess the price of wood is too low."

"We will have to think of a way of increasing the price then," said Numberlina. "But, from what you've told me, there's another reason."

"What's that?"

"Your father works hard and, although you're young and should be spending time at school, you help him as much as you can. Your stepmother does nothing. So your father and you are supporting a greedy, lazy person. Not only do you share with your stepmother, but she takes more than either of you. So we will have to do something about that."

"What can we do about anything?" asked Piff. "I've been thrown out. My father and stepmother have agreed I must leave home and stand on my own feet."

"I doubt that," said Numberlina. "Your stepmother has thrown you out and your father was too weak to stop her. We will go back to your home today and start to put things right."

"I don't think that will work," said Piff. "My stepmother will be angry if I return. Believe me, you don't want to be around when she's angry. And there's something else. She doesn't believe in fairies."

"That's not a problem," Numberlina assured Piff. "If she doesn't believe in fairies, she won't be able to see me. It's no coincidence that faith and fairies share the same first three letters. Are you ready?"

"Are you sure this is such a good idea?" Piff really couldn't see the point of going back.

"Absolutely," Numberlina replied. "Whatever the difficulties, as the abacus might say, you can always count on me."

"Why are you getting involved? Why are you so keen to help me?" asked Piff.

"That's simple. I'm a good fairy. And don't forget," Numberlina added, with a tinkling laugh, "I'm on 15%."

They talked for another half hour. Numberlina explained what they were going to do. Piff listened carefully to every word. Numberlina opened Piff's eyes to exciting possibilities.

"There are two kinds of humanites," Numberlina had said. "There are those who wait for life to happen; and there are those who make life happen. You are going to make life happen. And, if we have just a little luck, you'll be surprised what you can achieve."

10

They reached the woodcutter's cottage at lunchtime. Jack and Jill were eating bread. They saved their sausages for the evening meal.

As soon as Jill saw Piff, she leapt up. "What are you doing here? I thought I made it clear, there's no place for you with us, not anymore."

Jack on the other hand was so pleased to see his daughter that he got up to greet her.

"Sit!" Jill commanded, and Jack sank back on to his chair.

"We cannot afford to keep you, to clothe you and feed you," said Jill. "I thought I explained the situation to you yesterday and we agreed you would leave home and learn to stand on your own feet."

Jill was determined and Jack was too afraid of his wife to say anything, even though he loved his daughter. So Jill thought that was an end of the matter.

But she was wrong. What happened next took Jack by surprise and utterly astonished Jill.

"I am staying," said Piff. "The way we live is hopeless. We don't have enough money to live on. One of the reasons for our poverty is that only two of the three of us do any work. You are lazy," she addressed Jill. "You are a burden. We are going to have to put you to work. If all three of us work, we will have more money."

Jill was so astonished that she found it difficult to find the words to express her rage. "I cannot work," she screamed eventually. "I am not well enough to work. My quota of sausages is scarcely sufficient to keep body and soul together. How dare you?"

"Good," said Piff unperturbed. "I'm glad you brought up the issue of sausages. You are not only lazy, you are also fat. That is why you find it difficult to work. So to solve both problems, from now on sausages will be distributed according to the amount of work performed. We are, as a family, currently on four sausages. Obviously father should have two, because he does most of the work. I should have one because I help him. And we will let you have one sausage on the clear understanding that, until you start to work, we are giving you the one sausage as an act of charity. As you lose weight, you will be able to work and, eventually, you will be able to earn your sausage rather than relying on our generosity."

"How dare you?" Jill repeated; it was all she could manage. She then turned to Jack. "Are you going to allow your daughter to talk to me like that?"

"Well, dear," said Jack, a little uncertainly, "what she says does make a lot of sense."

"And that's just the beginning," said Piff. "There are two kinds of people. There are those who wait for life to happen; and there are those who make life happen. We are going to make life happen."

That afternoon Piff helped her father gather wood and chop it up into firewood. It was good to be with her father, helping him. Jill sat in the hut, fretting and fuming by turns, and wondering how she could possibly survive on one sausage a day.

11

That evening, after Jack had gone to bed and Jill had stayed in bed, having retired immediately after she had eaten her one sausage, Numberlina joined Piff by the fire in the cottage's living room.

"Jack and Jill like to go to bed early," Numberlina observed.

"Well, Father gets tired, working all day and eating only two sausages. And I think Jill has decided, if she can't eat, she'd like to sleep so that the hours when she is awake and hungry will be fewer."

Numberlina smiled. "Jill has much to learn. We have to turn her from a shirker into a worker. But, it's good they are in bed. We can talk freely. You have done well today. You have started to use numbers."

"Have I?"

"Of course," said Numberlina. "You related your sausage quota to the work performed and allocated the sausages accordingly. Four sausages: two for your dad because he does two-thirds of the work; one for you because you do one-third of the work; and one for Jill out of charity because no decent family allows anyone to starve."

Piff shrugged. "If you say so. I just thought it was obvious."

"Maths *is* obvious," said Numberlina. "So let's do some more obvious maths. How much does your father charge for a sack of firewood?"

"He charges 50 pennies," said Piff sadly. "We used to be able to sell a sack for 60 pennies but the price has dropped." (A penny was the currency of Numberland.)

"And how many pieces of firewood are there in a sack?"

"On average there are 50 pieces," said Piff.

"So you're charging 1 penny for each piece of firewood."

"That's right," said Piff.

"Can you think of any way we could get more for the wood?" Numberlina asked.

Piff thought hard but without success.

"We need to add value," said Numberlina. "We need to give the customers a benefit for which they will pay a little extra. Is there any way we could make the wood more attractive to the customer?"

Piff shrugged. "It's difficult to make a sack more attractive. The sacks are made of coarse material and they're very heavy when full of firewood. In fact, they're so heavy that it's a problem sometimes, especially for the women. It's often the women who buy the firewood because their men are at work."

Numberlina said nothing but made it clear she expected Piff to continue thinking.

"I suppose we could sell the wood in smaller sacks, except that the sacks cost money so we would lose money, unless we could charge for the extra sacks."

Still Numberlina waited.

"Unless we got rid of the sacks altogether and tied the firewood in small bundles," said Piff at last.

"Now you're talking!" said a delighted Numberlina. "Let's talk numbers."

"We could put the firewood in bundles of 10," said Piff. "That means we could make 5 bundles out of each sackful. If we tied the bundles together with string, we would save on the cost of a sack."

"And, because you have added value, because you have made the buying of firewood easier, easier to order in smaller quantities, easier to carry if a full sack is too heavy, you can charge a little extra, say 12p a bundle. That would give you 60p for 50 pieces of firewood, instead of 50p for a sackful. What's more, Jill can help. No doubt she reckons a sack full of firewood is too heavy for her to handle but she can certainly make up the bundles of 10 and tie them. And the string to tie them will be cheaper than a sack, so there's a bit of a saving there."

12

The following morning, Piff announced her plan. Jack was not very keen. He said that he had always sold the firewood in sacks and everyone was used to buying their firewood in sacks. He just didn't like the idea of change.

Jill was more emphatically hostile for obvious reasons. From the day she had married Jack, she had never lifted a finger to help him in his work and she had loaded as much of the housework as she could on to Piff. Now her stepdaughter, whom she had hoped she would never see again, was suggesting she should spend her days selecting and binding together bundles of firewood. She immediately presented a number of objections. The work would be too hard; her hands were too delicate to handle wood; she would get dirty, dusty and utterly exhausted. In short, the work would kill her.

This last argument carried rather less weight with Piff than Jill had hoped.

"We must give the idea a try," insisted Piff. "If it is successful, we will have 60 pennies for the equivalent of a sackful of wood, instead of 50 pennies and we will save on the cost of sacks which is more than the cost of the string. We will be able to have more sausages. If Jack has more food, he will be able to work harder and gather more wood. If we sell more wood, at 12 pennies for 10 sticks, we will have more money than we have ever had. And you, dear Stepmother, will be able to eat sausages until they come out of your fat bottom."

"You mustn't talk to your mother like that," said Jack.

"She's not my mother," Piff retorted.

Jack and Jill looked at Piff in astonishment. She had always been a polite little girl, generally doing as she was told without complaint. They didn't recognise this determined, strong-willed young lady. Jack felt rather proud and Jill felt cowed.

"I suppose we could give it a try," said Jack. "You could wear gloves to protect your hands and take the work slowly at the beginning," he suggested to Jill.

Jill remained unconvinced.

"Let's put it this way," said Piff. "The sausage allocation is now based on the amount of work performed. If you ever want to eat more than the one sausage you are allocated out of charity, you are going to have to pull your very considerable weight."

After tasting the delights of the food provided by Numberlina, Piff herself no longer saw the Numberland sausage as the height of culinary perfection. But, for Jill, it was very much life's main attraction. The threat of permanent hunger, combined with the possibility of an increased sausage quota, forced Jill into line.

"We start tomorrow," said Piff, in a tone that discouraged disagreement.

13

The following day, Jill was put to work preparing bundles of 10 pieces of firewood. She grumbled almost continuously but, since Jack and Piff left for the village market as soon as they had drunk their glass of befangle juice, there was no one to hear her complaints.

Numberlina returned to the fairy dome and summoned an extraordinary general meeting of the numbers. By the way, any disagreement about which of the numbers was more important had long ago been satisfactorily resolved. Although some rivalry persisted, they had all agreed that each number had its own unique properties and there was no point in arguing that any particular number was more important than another.

"We are all one family," One had finally concluded on behalf of the odd numbers.

Two had agreed. "Different but equal," she said.

"If ever there was a time when you must all cooperate, it's now," said Numberlina. "We have work to do.

The woodcutter's daughter needs our help and we must give it to her. I believe she is the one who can overthrow Prince Baltigral and help us to get the better of the Anathemath."

Such a claim, that Piff could be the saviour of the land, sent a tsunami of excitement through the numbers. Nought, who was generally reticent, had so far said nothing but was now moved to speak. Unfortunately, once Nought started, he was difficult to stop.

"Let us combine our strength. I am nothing, but as you know, when I join any of you, I can increase your power ten times over. I can make One, 10, and then 100 and then 1,000. I can make any of you more powerful than you can possibly imagine. Let our enemies muster armies as vast as those that the Persians brought against the Greeks in ancient times and, with my help, you shall outnumber them. Yet I am nothing. I am the paradox that can solve life's deepest mysteries. I am before the beginning of numbers; yet I am in the middle of numbers. For every positive number, there is a negative number and, when the positive and negative meet, there is nothing, always nothing, however large or small the positive number and its negative counterpart may be, bring them together and there am I, there is nothing…"

Nought intended to carry on in this vein indefinitely but Numberlina cut him short.

"Thank you, Nought," said Numberlina. "Good to know you're fully on board and with the programme. Now, what we need to do today is a little bit of number crunching."

I should perhaps explain that number crunching has a particular meaning in Numblish. It certainly doesn't mean knocking numbers together, beating them into submission or processing them through a machine in some way. Number crunching in Numblish means persuading numbers to work together to achieve a common goal. Probably the best analogy is the scrum in a game of rugby. The numbers have to bind together into a powerful many-legged, many-armed body in order to drive forward.

"I've gathered all the information we need from Piff. Now, with your help, I can do the maths."

I don't need to bore you with all the details but I do need to tell you what "do the maths" meant. Piff had explained all the costs the woodcutter and his family had to pay every day and the amount of money the woodcutter earned each day from selling wood.

It's fairly obvious to everyone (except of course human governments and banks and some really very stupid people) that you always need more money coming in than going out. Jack might not have been the sharpest saw in the woodcutter's toolbox, but even he knew that you can't keep spending more than you earn. Hence the cutback in the sausage quota!

Numberlina knew all the woodcutter's costs (for sausages, bread, befangle juice, rent, sacks, string and other odds and ends). And she knew how much wood he sold. So she was able to construct a spreadsheet, with all the data on costs and income so she could see exactly what happened if a cost or the income went up or down.

"Whoa!" I hear you say. "You're talking about a computer spreadsheet. That's a routine application on a human computer. That's a human invention. Not something a fairy would have."

Well I say "Whoa!" back to you. Long before Khufu built his pyramid, fairies were using sheets, covered in squares, spread out on the ground for performing essential calculations, such as the optimum beat of a fairy's wings to achieve a perfect balance between speed and distance, or the quickest path between here and there. I have to say the compulsion of humanites (as the fairies call humans) to claim they have invented everything, particularly prevalent amongst the folk living just north of Numberland, can be intensely irritating.

No matter. Numberlina had spread her sheet which, fully extended, more or less covered the dining table provided for human guests. Then, when she had performed all the necessary calculations, she was delighted to see that, with Jack's current sales of 200 pieces of firewood a day, if they switched from sacks to string and sold the wood at the same price as before, and stayed with the four sausage a day diet, they could convert, after tax, a loss of 2 pennies a day to a profit of 8 pennies. Not much, perhaps, but a profit, not a loss.

Numberlina also calculated the daily profit if Jack could just sell 50 more pieces of firewood each day. He would then have a profit of 33 pennies a day.

(Yes, I know, number crunching can be a bit tedious for most humans. For the numbers themselves, however, it was what they were all about, so, in deference to the numbers and the minority of humans with an interest in such matters, we include, with Numberlina's kind permission, some of her actual worksheets, relating to this and all subsequent calculations at the end of this book. Best ignored, in my opinion.)

14

That evening, Numberlina returned to the woodcutter's hut to check on progress.

Piff and Jack had sold four sacks of wood at the village market.

Jill had spent the day counting out 10 pieces of firewood and tying them into neat bundles. It would be wrong to say that Jill had been happy in her work. Although she had worn gloves, some splinters had penetrated the fabric and embedded themselves in hands which previously had never done an honest day's work. So Jill was tired and her hands were sore but, on the positive side, she noticed two things. First, work had taken her mind off food, at least for most of the time. Secondly, she couldn't help but feel some pride in making a contribution to the common good. Her sausage that evening would have been well and truly earned.

"How was it, dear?" Jack had asked Jill when he and Piff had returned. "You've done awfully well," he added, looking at the stacked bundles of firewood.

"I am not accustomed to this type of work," said Jill.

"You're not accustomed to any type of work," said Piff. "But you seem to have done a good job and your work rate will improve with practice."

After the evening meal, Jack and Jill retired to bed. Jill was completely exhausted by her efforts and Jack was weakened by unremitting labour on a limited diet.

As soon as they were gone, Numberlina started to tell Piff of her calculations.

"If we take all your costs into account, you ended today with a loss of 2 pennies," Numberlina explained.

"Thanks a bundle," said Piff. "You mean that after all three of us have put in a day's work, and eaten only four sausages altogether, we still made a loss."

"Yes, but tomorrow, if you sell the same amount of wood at the same price but in bundles tied with string, you will make a profit of 8 pennies."

"How do you reckon that?" asked Piff.

"Because 10 bits of string are quite a bit cheaper than a sack," Numberlina explained. "A profit of 8 pennies may not be much but many a mickle makes a muckle. What's more, if you charge 12 pennies a bundle, instead of 10 pennies, you will make a much bigger profit for the day. Do you know what that means? If you can sell those extra bundles, you can go back to eating eight sausages a day and still have a profit of 8 pennies."

"How do you know all this?" asked Piff, surprised at the speed of her calculations.

"Numbers, my dear Piff, numbers," said Numberlina. "Get them on your side and you can conquer the world. We fairies of the Numerati have a saying. You will not understand it now, but one day, it will be clear to you:

Add, you grow stronger; take away what you need.
Multiply, you are legion; divide and succeed.

Now, before you go for a well-earned sleep, do you have any other questions?"

"Yes," said Piff yawning. "What's a muckle?"

15

When Piff and Jack returned from the village market the next day, they were excited.

The bundles of wood had turned out to be exceedingly popular. Sacks of firewood were heavy. The stronger men could manage to swing them on to their carts but they were too heavy for most women. And the heavy sacks were a nuisance when the customer reached home. The bundles were much easier to handle and, indeed, to bring into the home for burning.

In any case, many customers didn't want to buy a whole sack. A whole sackful was expensive, a lot of money to hand over in a single dollop. Many of the villagers liked the idea of buying the wood they needed when they needed it. Jack and Piff had found no difficulty in selling 20 bundles of wood, the equivalent of 4 sacksful, at a price of 12 pennies a bundle.

Jack and Piff knew they had done well but it was only after Jack and Jill had retired that Numberlina informed Piff she had made a profit of 28 pennies.

"But we sold the same amount of wood as usual," said an astonished Piff. "And you said we usually lose a couple of pennies."

"Yes, but you saved a bit of cost on changing from sacksful to bundles, and then you sold the 50 pieces (an old sackful) for 60 pennies, rather than 50 pennies. Believe me, I'm right. When Numberlina does the maths, the maths get well and truly done."

At this point Numberlina did a little jig in the air. *"No going back, Jack,"* she sang. *"We're up the hill, Jill. Get a whiff, young Piff, take a sniff of success, oh yes; I'm not guessing; you can take it, we will make it; be bold, go for gold; be a smarty, join the party, you must trust the Numerati."*

Piff was alarmed. Numberlina seemed to have gone a tad mad.

"I'm fine," said Numberlina. "Just for a moment, I was away with the fairies."

16

The following day, Jack and Piff spent the morning cutting and gathering wood, while Jill, still reluctant and complaining, sat and bound bundles of 10 pieces of firewood together with string.

After eating a lunch of bread and befangle juice, Jack and Piff set out for the village market. This time they took 25 bundles of wood, the equivalent of 5 sacksful. It was a long afternoon, but by the time the market was closing down, they had sold all 25 bundles. And they had sold them all at 12p a bundle.

When, the evening after dinner in the cottage, Numberlina and Piff settled down to review the day's takings, Numberlina announced a profit of 58 pennies.

"That's more than we've ever made," said Piff. "What would happen if we started to eat eight sausages a day, as we used to?"

"Numberlina laughed. "You could eat eight sausages a day and still make a profit of 38 pennies but I suggest you go back to seven sausages a day, not eight. On seven sausages a day, each of you will have one more sausage. Jack will be on three sausages; you and Jill will be on two. Jack will no longer be hungry and can work harder. Jill will be much relieved to see her sausage quota doubled and will at last recognise the connection between effort and reward. And you, young Piff, deserve two sausages and more. And, on a ration of seven sausages a day, you will be making 43 pennies profit a day."

"I don't know how to thank you," said Piff. "You've put my family back on its feet."

"Nonsense," said Numberlina sharply. "First of all, you deserve the credit for this modest improvement in your family's circumstances. Secondly, this is not time for thanks and congratulation. We've hardly started. How can we increase the income?"

Piff was taken aback. "Well, I don't think there is anything else we can do. The villagers won't buy more than 25 bundles a day. It was quite hard to get rid of the last few."

"So?" Numberlina prompted.

Piff frowned.

"Is your local village the only village in the forest?" asked Numberlina.

"No, of course not," said Piff, "there are a dozen villages in this forest as you know – but we can only sell to one village."

"And why is that?" asked Numberlina.

"We have only one cart," said Piff lamely.

"Could you not load the cart with enough bundles for two villages, say 50 bundles," suggested Numberlina. "The two of you could drive to your local village. There, Jack could drop you and 25 bundles off, and then he could go on to the next village with the remaining 25 bundles. When he's finished, he could pick you up on the way back."

Piff thought for a minute. "It's possible," she conceded.

"If you sold all 50 bundles, and kept to your ration of seven sausages, you would make a profit of 193 pennies a day."

Piff looked at Numberlina with amazement. On a daily profit of 193 pennies a day, they would be the richest family in their part of the forest, richer than all the households in their local village.

Numberlina continued: "I promised to make you rich and I will keep my word but we need to aim high. You promised me a 15% share of the gold you earn. We are still talking pennies. We need a plan to earn so many pennies that we start to measure our income in gold. *I've no wish to scold but I'm sure you've been told; it's time to be bold; more wood must be sold, pennies to gold, before you're too old! I have to confess, I won't settle for less. Share my itches for riches. The sky is the limit; we're in it to win it. Less dreaming; more scheming! Are you gleaning my meaning?*"

"I think so," said Piff, eager to stop Numberlina's torrent of rhymes. A few days ago, she had been alone and crying in the forest, an outcast from her penniless family. Now, with Numberlina's help, she was in charge of her family and on the way to a wealthy future. There was a price to pay. They would have to work hard, harder than before. They would have to employ people to help with the work. But the rewards would be great. For the first time in her life, Piff understood what "making life happen" meant.

17

Within three weeks, Piff was employing ten people and providing wood to all ten villages in the forest. Jack was now general manager and, when not busy organising the employees and their cartloads of wood, he gave Jill a hand with tying up the bundles of wood for their local village. Jill, still working all day on wood bundling, was now losing weight, despite her increased sausage allocation. Strangely, as she became thinner, her temper improved.

The employees were paid 100p a day, which was the going rate for a day's labour. Each employee had to gather wood in the forest around where they lived and provide their own horse and cart, for which Piff paid them an extra 40p a day to cover the hire charge. Piff and Jack were now selling 250 bundles of wood a day. And making a profit of 671 pennies a day, or 4,697 pennies a week!

It's worth mentioning the contribution Numberlina made to planning the routes that each of the employees took on their necessary journeys from forest to village and from their homes to the woodcutter's cottage. Numberlina gave Piff a clever device which, when attached to a wagon wheel, counted the number of wheel rotations on a journey.

"It's very clever," Piff had said. "But what's it for? What use is it?"

"Well it means we can work out how far each of the employees has to travel and we can tell them which are the shortest routes. And that means we can make sure the 40p allowance for the wagon is fair and we can help the employees to be more efficient."

"That would be good," Piff had agreed. "But how does counting wheel rotations tell us all that?"

"If we know the number of rotations, we know the distance travelled."

"Do we?" said Piff, unconvinced.

"If we know how many times the circumference of the wheel, that's the outer rim of the wheel, has passed over the ground, we know the distance the cart has travelled."

"Do we?" Piff repeated. "How do we know the length of the rim of the wheel? It would be difficult to measure with a straight ruler and, if we make even a small error, that error would increase with every turn of the wheel."

"Aha," said Numberlina. "I think it's time for Pi."

Piff frowned. "I'm not hungry."

Numberlina laughed. "No not pie, *Pi*. Pi is a magic number. Humanites call them irrational numbers but they are really numbers devised by fairies to make life easier and, in some cases, even to make life make sense. Pi tells you how to measure a circumference of a circle. All you have to do is measure the diameter of the wheel (that's the width of the wheel if you draw a line through its centre) and multiply it by Pi."

"But what is Pi?" Piff asked.

"It's 3.14159265358979323846264338327950... to 32 decimal places. In fact the decimal places go on for ever."

"I think I'd rather take a guess," said Piff. She had never been a great fan of long or, as in this case, interminable multiplication.

Numberlina calmed Piff's fears. "Don't worry. Three decimal places will do. If the diameter of the wheel is half a metre, we multiply 0.5 x 3.142 which gives us 1.571 – which means the circumference of the wheel is 1 metre and 57 centimetres. If, on a particular journey, the wheel has turned 1,000 times, we know the distance travelled is 1.57 x 1,000 = 1,570 metres."

"That's really clever," said Piff. "It means we can plan routes through the forest, instead of doing everything by guesswork. So where did this Pi come from?"

Numberlina adopted a serious expression. "Pi goes back to ancient times. The Egyptians had a fairly good idea, at least to a couple of decimal places and, later, around AD 500, the Chinese worked it out to seven decimal places. Eventually, mankind realised that Pi was not as most other numbers. The decimal series after the 3 is infinite and non-recurring. In other words," Numberlina concluded proudly, "it's one of ours."

"One of yours?" queried Piff.

"We devised it long before the Egyptians. We need it to measure out our fairy circles. Fairy circles have to be a precise size. In your form of measurement, they must have a circumference of 999 centimetres, or any multiple of 999. All we had to do was divide 999 by 3.141592 = 318cms to find the diameter. We then divided the diameter by 2 = 159cms to get the radius. We could then drive a stick into the ground, attach a rope 159cms long to the stick and use the other end to mark out a circle with the circumference of 999cms. If we needed a larger circle, say 3 times the size, with a circumference of 2.997 metres, we just increased the length of the rope three times, to 477cms."

"I'm impressed," Piff conceded.

"Good," said Numberlina. "Never underestimate the importance of numbers or the power of the Numerati. And never doubt how much they can help you."

With the benefit of improved journey planning, at the end of the first year, Piff had a profit of 244,062 pennies.

Throughout the first year, Numberlina would visit the woodcutter's cottage every month when the moon was full and she and Piff would discuss the business. Piff was in charge of the money but Numberlina did all the figure-work. To calculate income, costs and profit, Numberlina always brought along her faithful fairy spreadsheet which she laid out on a table or on the forest's ferny floor for Piff to study. Piff was a quick learner and soon began to enjoy working with figures. She had never seen the point of maths before but now they were counting money, she saw how important numbers could be.

On the day of Piff's 15th birthday, which happened to be a full moon, Numberlina arrived in the evening for their monthly chat.

"Happy birthday, Piff," said Numberlina, as she landed on the small wooden porch of the woodcutter's cottage. It was a warm, late July evening and Piff was enjoying the rustling sound of the gentle breeze playing with the shimmering silver leaves in the moonlight. "You have done really well in our first year."

"It's been amazing," said Piff. "Sometimes I just can't believe it. It's been hard work but we were poor and now we're rich. I don't know how I can ever repay you."

"That's easy," said Numberlina with a smile. "I've checked the gold price today and one gold coin is worth 3,050 pennies. That means you have a profit of 80 gold coins. 15% of 80 is 12. So 12 gold coins is an excellent, thank you."

Piff happily agreed to Numberlina's commission. Numberlina's fee of 35,517 pennies was far more reasonable than the 50% of profits demanded by the rapacious Prince Baltigral. Piff and her family had actually made a profit before tax of 580,580 pennies, of which Baltigral had taken 290,290 pennies.

"Now," said Numberlina, "I want you to meet three of my friends. I'm hoping they will be able to help you in the coming year. First, number Seven."

From behind one of the trees at the edge of the clearing stepped Seven. Less than a metre tall, Seven was smartly dressed in a well-tailored suit of green. On his head, he wore a pork-pie hat in which, inserted at a jaunty angle, was a feather wafting gently in the breeze. "Hi, there, Piff," he said, with a smile and a wink. "You're a real cutey."

Piff was none too happy with the familiarity but she couldn't help herself smiling at this cocky little fellow, less than half her size, calling her cute.

"You'll find her more astute than cute," said Numberlina, rebuking Seven. Then turning to Piff, she added, "Seven is quick-witted and smart. He has a good eye for an opportunity. And he is lucky. He should help us in developing our business."

Another number stepped forward. "And this," Numberlina continued, "is Nine." Nine, dressed in a plain but well-cut suit, was a little taller than Seven. With cool, grey eyes, high cheekbones and a firm chin, he exuded a quiet confidence. "I'm delighted to meet you," said Nine, taking Piff's hand and making a short bow. "If I can help in any way, it will be my pleasure."

"Nine is highly-regarded by the other numbers and by humanites alike," Numberlina confided. "Without any flattery, I can say that Nine is extremely intelligent and, as the square of Three, brings a high level of sophistication to the table."

Piff momentarily wondered what Numberlina meant by 'bringing something to the table', given there was no table, but she let it pass.

"Finally, I should like to introduce Nought," said Numberlina, "or rather allow Nought to introduce himself."

"I am more than much," Nought began, "and yet I am nothing. From hero to zero in the twinkling of an eye! I am perfectly formed, although I am before the first to concede that beauty is in the eye of the beholder. Whether we are talking money or men, once you make a start, I will be there to increase the numbers tenfold, over and over again. Nothing shall come of nothing but there is no end to what nothing will become, given the slightest encouragement…"

Numberlina gently interrupted. "Nought has his problems but he will be invaluable when we want to scale up the operation."

Piff patted Nought on the head which calmed him. "He seems a little unsure of himself," observed Piff.

"He is," Numberlina confirmed. "But don't underestimate Nought. True, he has issues but the part he plays in the world of numbers is incalculable. He has a special place in the esteem of the Numerati."

Again Piff wondered who the Numerati were but, before she could ask, Numberlina made an announcement. "Seven, Nine and Nought have something they wish to say."

Seven, Nine and Nought were amusing themselves with a little number play and failed to hear Numberlina's cue.

"I suppose you two realise that 907 is a prime number," said Nine to his companions.

"As is 709," said Seven, not to be out done by Nine.

"But had either of you realised," enquired Nought, "that 790 and 970 are both the product of three primes, two of whom, sadly not here today, are members of our elite single digit band. If 79 is multiplied by Two and Five you have 790; and if 97 is multiplied by Two and Five you get 970."

"Come on, chaps," Numberlina gently interrupted. She knew how much the numbers liked to play but she had brought them with her for a purpose. "Do your thing and sing," she instructed.

The three numbers cleared their throats and then sang "Happy Birthday" in a surprisingly harmonious manner. Then Seven spoke. "Numberlina and all the numbers from Nought to Nine wish you the happiest of birthdays and the most successful of years. And we give you this gift."

Piff took the small box that Seven offered her. She opened the box. Inside was a gold chain and, hanging on it was a circle of gold no more than two centimetres in diameter. Within the circle, was a pentagram, attached to the circle at three points. The top section of the pentagram had been converted into a set of perfectly balanced scales. It was a fine piece of work. Piff put the chain over her head and hung the medallion round her neck. "It's beautiful," she said, "and so kind of you."

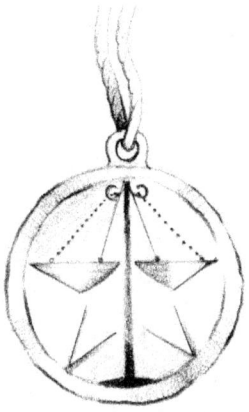

It was the first piece of jewellery anyone had ever given her.

"The pentagram has a special meaning for the Numerati," said Numberlina, "and the scales will have a special meaning for you. I shall tell you more another day." Before Piff could ask her to explain, Numberlina declared: "Tomorrow, we shall begin to make plans for the coming year."

18

In his palace in Old Hexam, the capital of Numberland, Prince Baltigral was reviewing the tax receipts for the last year. Times were hard and the revenues had scarcely risen over the last few years, despite substantial tax increases.

"This is no good," he barked at Chancellor Redring. "Revenues are flat or declining. We shall have to increase taxes."

"You know me," said the Chancellor, "always more than happy to whack up taxes but I have to tell you that we are at the very limit. If we increase taxes any more, the rich will leave and the poor will starve. Revenues will decline rather than increase."

"There's not much point in having a Chancellor," said Prince Baltigral in his most menacing voice, "if all you do is tell me what can't be done. Did I not send you on that motivation course entitled: '*Yes if…*', not '*No because…*'? If you cannot come up with more positive counsel, I shall be tempted to cancel my counsellor."

Redring knew well enough what 'cancel' meant in this context. He loosened the collar of his shirt nervously.

"There is one glimmer of hope on the horizon," said Redring hastily. "Surprisingly, there is a part of the forest that has returned substantially increased tax revenues compared with the previous year. It seems the woodcutter Jack, with the help of his daughter Stephanie, known locally as Piff, has organised some kind of collective and, by all accounts, including theirs, things seem to be going rather well."

"Then I suggest you investigate," growled Prince Baltigral. "And report back sharpish. We need to know what our more innovative and industrious citizens are up to. We may not be able to impose higher taxes on everyone but it makes sense to take more from those who can afford it, especially if they can't move away – and, as far as I can recall, the forest, which I assume is the source of their wealth, is a fixed asset."

"He's not very good," said a voice behind the prince's left shoulder.

The source of this criticism of Redring was none other than the Anathemath, unseen and unheard by all except the prince.

At this point, dear reader, I need a little understanding from you. No doubt, since he plays an important part in this story, you would like a description of the Anathemath, however cursory. And it's a reasonable request. After all, I am the storyteller and I have complete control of events and, indeed, all the words in the English and Numblish languages to call upon.

And yet, unfortunately, I cannot describe the Anathemath. Why? Because he is indescribable. Although I call him 'he', I am not even sure whether he is male or female or neither. He is more substantial than a cloud, a cloud of greenish hue, but certainly less defined than a person, more a shadow than a man. Some swear he has only one eye which is his most obvious distinguishing feature but I cannot vouch for the truth of it. All I can say for sure is that he is clever and he sells his services to those in power. What does he do? He helps the powerful to keep their power by muddling the minds of those whom the powerful rule. Forgive me. All will become clear as this story proceeds.

19

On the day after her birthday, Piff called a meeting. Present were Numberlina, Seven, Nine and Nought. Before the meeting began, Seven and Nine were yet again indulging in typical number chat.

"It's interesting," observed Nine, "that whichever way you combine us, you end up with a prime number, 79 or 97."

"True," Seven replied, with an impish smile, "but I am a prime in my own right and you, friend Nine, are not."

Nine paused for a moment. He really enjoyed his battles with Seven. "True," he conceded, "but I am a square, the square of Three which is the very first odd-number prime. So you could say I'm full of primes. What's more, if you multiply me by any number from 1 to 10 and add the digits in the result together, you come back to me, Nine. What's more, if you multiply me by any number and add the digits together in the result over and over again, in the end you will come back to me. That's special, really special and that's not something you can claim. Go on, pick a number, any number."

"OK," said Seven, tipping back his pork-pie hat and winking at Numberlina, "how about 7,777?"

"Fine," said Nine. "If I multiply that number by 9, the result is…" At this point he tailed off.

"You will get 69,993," said Numberlina helpfully, knowing Nine would have some difficulty in calculating such a large number. "And, if you add those numbers together, you get 36. And if you add 3 and 6, you get 9."

"And," added Nine with some degree of complacency, "you will notice that, in the middle of the result, 69,993, there just happens to be the sacred number 999, and that the two outside numbers, 6 and 3, add up to 9. It's not at all surprising that, when humans wish to look their smartest, it is said they are 'dressed up to the nines'."

"I'm not entirely sure what that proves," Seven grinned, unabashed, "except perhaps that you're just a little self-obsessed, a bit like One."

"If you multiply anything by me," offered Nought helpfully, "you get me, which is just as clever as Nine but with a lot less effort."

Numberlina clapped her hands. There was nothing she loved more than this badinage between numbers.

Piff, on the other hand was less amused. "Enough," she said. "We have important matters to discuss."

Numberlina gently rebuked Piff. "These are numbers, Piff. Just like people, they like to talk about the things they have done or plan to do. They like to boast a little about their accomplishments. Of course it's boring for everyone else but, for them, it's the most interesting thing in the world. Given how much we need their help, I think we have to be a little indulgent and forgiving."

"Fine," said Piff. "I understand but I have a busy day ahead of me and I've got some big ideas to discuss."

Numberlina and the three numbers quietened down.

"We are doing well, selling firewood," Piff began, "but I don't see how we can grow the business any further. We are selling all the firewood the villagers need and our operation now covers all the forest we can reach. If we are to expand, we need to think of something new."

"What are our strengths?" asked Numberlina.

"We all work hard," said Piff. "Even my stepmother is putting in some effort."

"What else?"

"We have learned much over the last year about selling and pricing and managing money," Piff replied.

"Excellent," said Numberlina.

"And you have wood," said Nine.

"Yes, of course we have wood," Piff responded. "We live in a forest." And then she stopped. No one said anything. Then Piff continued, "Yes, we have wood. We gather it, sell it and our customers burn it. They sit around their fires and they burn the wood."

"And what do they sit on?" asked Nine and Seven together, knowing what Piff was thinking.

"Chairs, wooden chairs," said Piff with a laugh. "They sit on wooden chairs; they eat at wooden tables; and they sleep on wooden beds."

"*On the money, honey!*" Numberlina exclaimed delightedly. "You can add value to the wood by making it into furniture, instead of burning it. You will have to learn how to cut the trees and saw them up; how to store the wood to season it; how to work it. But you will find carpenters in Old Hexam. At the beginning, they can make your furniture. Then they can train the villagers. It will be a real challenge but, if you succeed, this new business will make you truly wealthy, rather than just well off."

20

When the money from her firewood business had begun to pour in, Piff had decided to improve her family's living accommodation.

"I can help with that," said Numberlina. "You need to have a design that ensures any additions or extensions to your cottage are in the right proportion. For that, you will need perhaps the finest of all the fairy numbers – the Golden Mean."

"And what is that?" Piff had learned to pay attention to Numberlina's enthusiastic explanations of fairy numbers. They always turned out to be more interesting and useful than she expected.

"The Golden Mean is a number that can perform wonders in mathematics, and one that plays a part throughout nature and creation. That number, to three decimal places, is 1.618 and we call it Phi. Phi (Φ), like Pi (Π), is an irrational number which means that the series of numbers after decimal point goes on for ever and never repeats a sequence."

"So how does this Golden Mean work?" asked Piff.

"If you divide a line in two so that the ratio between the whole line and the bigger of the two parts is exactly the same as the ratio between the bigger part and the smaller part, you have the Golden Mean.

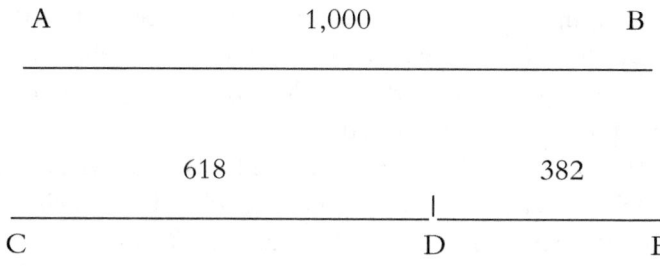

AB must be 1.618 the length of CD
CD must be 1.618 the length of DE

$$1{,}000/618 = 1.618 \quad 618/382 = 1.618$$
$$618 + 382 = 1{,}000$$

"That proportion – in a line, or in a solid, or in a building, or in living forms – is pleasing to the eye."

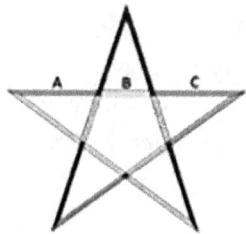

"The most sacred symbol for the Numerati," Numberlina continued enthusiastically, "is the pentagram. That's why we gave you the medallion for your birthday. The pentagram is a fine example of the Golden Mean. Each side of the pentagram is intersected by two other sides at points that split the side into Golden Mean ratios." With a few strokes of her wand, Numberlina created a pentagram floating in the air. "If you take the line ABC, C is in the same ratio to AB, as AB is to ABC; and A is in the same ratio to BC as BC is to ABC. All five lines of the pentagram are intersected in this way."

"And you're saying the Golden Mean can be used in house building?" Piff queried.

"Absolutely," said Numberlina. "The Golden Mean was used for such a purpose by the ancients. Phidias, the architect of the Parthenon in ancient Athens, used the Golden Mean to ensure the perfect proportions of his temple to Athena. Before that, the Egyptians used it in constructing the pyramids. And before that, nature used it in determining the form of plants. The uses of the Golden Mean are without number, so to speak. Like Pi, Phi is another triumph of the Numerati."

"Fascinating," said Piff, "but how do I apply the Golden Mean to this cottage?"

"That's easy," Numberlina replied. "Give me your rough drawings to show the space you need and I will use my fairy spreadsheet to generate architects drawings. We will ensure that each addition and the building as a whole complies with the rules of the Golden Mean. Then, for sure, all will be harmonious and beautiful as well as eminently functional. Oh yes," said Numberlina, warming to her theme, "the fairies specialising in construction *are good with wood, slick with brick, great with slate – and always do what they oughta with mortar.*"

"Enough!" said Piff.

21

Shortly after Piff's 15th birthday, Chancellor Redring paid the woodcutter a visit. He was immediately struck by the hive of building activity around the cottage.

Jack greeted his unexpected guest as best he could but he was intimidated by the arrival of such an important man, in such expensive clothes, in such a grand carriage.

"I am Redring, Chancellor of Numberland, and I have come from the Court of Prince Baltigral in the Palace in Old Hexam. I am here to talk with the manager of the firewood business."

"That would be me. I am Jack, the woodcutter," said Jack uncertainly. Piff had given him the title of manager of the firewood business but he knew he was not well-equipped to deal with a person of such high status. He should have explained that Piff took all the decisions and that he was more a supervisor of the workers than a manager of the enterprise but he didn't. He was rather flattered to be considered sufficiently important to converse with the Chancellor of the county.

"Well, Jack the Woodcutter, you and I need to have a little chat," said Redring. "First, let me say how pleased Prince Baltigral has been with your tax returns. Unlike most of his other subjects, you have met his expectations."

Jack began to relax a little.

"So how's business now?" asked Redring, casually.

"We're doing really well," said Jack. "We are properly organised. Our employees gather wood first thing in the morning in their own patch of the forest. Their wives select and bind the wood in bundles. Then the men sell the wood in the local markets in the afternoon. We pay for the horse and cart they need. It took some time to sort out but now everything is running smoothly."

"Excellent," said Redring. "So this year's sales could be as good, or better, than those last year?"

"I'd say better," said Jack. He was proud of the system Piff had set up and he assumed sales would grow as they had in the past. Unlike Piff, he hadn't taken into account that they were already selling all the firewood the foresters needed.

"In that case, I'm sure you will be comfortable with a modest increase in the rent, shall we say double, and a slight increase in tax, say from 50% to 60%."

Jack didn't know what to say. So he said nothing.

When he told Piff what had happened, she had not been angry, but she had made him promise never to talk to anyone from the prince's court again.

Numberlina was rather less forgiving. That evening, she spread her sheet on the forest floor, checked the numbers and announced to Piff: "In addition to what we already pay the exceedingly greedy Prince Baltigral, your father has just agreed to hand over more than a quarter of our profits."

Piff shrugged. "I've spoken to him. He won't do it again."

"That's a relief," said Numberlina huffily. She was on a percentage, so Jack had given away not only Piff's money, but hers too.

22

It took three years to launch the furniture business. In those three years, Jack and Jill managed the firewood business. Piff used all the profits to finance the development programme. The profit from the firewood averaged 150,000 pennies a year (after Numberlina's 15% take and other increased costs, i.e. rent and tax), so at the end of three years, Piff had ploughed some 450,000 pennies into the furniture development project.

In the development work, Piff was helped by all the numbers who worked as hard as Piff herself to get the new project off the ground.

The designs for the furniture were simple but sturdy, ideal for the requirements of the village folk. Piff discovered almost immediately the importance of numbers in making even the simplest furniture. A table needed precisely shaped corners to make a square or rectangular shape. When the trainee villagers tried to cut the wood by eye, the results were always a little misshapen, until Three, Four and Five offered to help.

"How can they help?" Piff had asked irritably. She had been trying for weeks to find a way of consistently cutting the wood at right angles.

"It's simple," said Numberlina. "If you draw a triangle with the sides measuring 3, 4, and 5, the angle opposite the 5 will be a perfect right angle."

Piff frowned. She drew a triangle as Numberlina had described. "Why does that work?" she asked.

Four answered. "It's all about squares."

"I know that," said Piff. "We need to make perfectly square corners for our tables and beds and benches. What I was asking was why the triangle thing works."

Four was a little upset by Piff's dismissive tone. Four was rather proud of her central role in constructing right angled triangles, not to mention her acknowledged status as the first square number, if you exclude 1 which, squared, is still 1 and 0 which, squared, is still 0.

"You misunderstand," said Four, puffing up her plump cheeks indignantly. "I mean it's all about square numbers. The square of 3 is 9. The square of 4 is 16. And the square of 5 is 25. If you add 9 and 16, you get 25. Whenever the square of the length of two sides of a triangle add up to the square of the length of the third, the angle opposite the third side will be a right angle. As it happens, 3, 4 and 5 is the simplest combination to produce a right angle triangle but you can use any multiple of 3, 4 and 5; for example 6, 8 and 10 (36 + 64 = 100)."

"Or other sets of numbers," Numberlina chimed in, "where the squares of the two smaller numbers add up to the square of the bigger number; for example 5, 12, 13 (25 + 144 = 169) - but 3, 4 and 5 is the neatest set."

"That's amazing," said Piff.
"That's geometry," said Four.
"That's the power of numbers," said Numberlina.

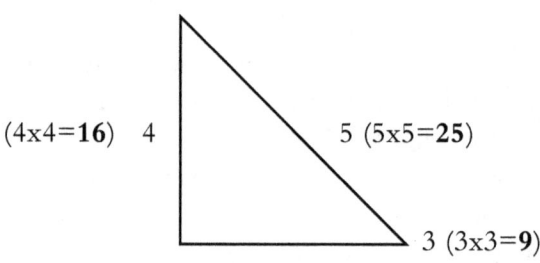

Perfect right angle
9 + 16 = 25

23

When Chancellor Redring returned to the palace, he expected that Prince Baltigral would be pleased with his report.

"I've doubled the rent and upped the tax on their profits from 50% to 60%," he declared. "That should bring in an additional 65,000 pennies, give or take."

"And they are happy with the new arrangements?" enquired Baltigral languidly. Obviously he didn't care in the slightest whether his subjects were happy to pay their rent or their taxes. Indeed, most people dislike paying both, and increases in either are never well received. No, he was simply keeping the conversation going long enough for the Anathemath to express an opinion.

"Ask him if he noticed anything unusual in the course of his visit," said the shadow behind Prince Baltigral's left shoulder.

The prince asked, as instructed.

"Only that they seemed to be in the middle of some

building work," Redring replied.

"Ask him whom he dealt with on his visit," instructed the Anathemath.

Baltigral asked and Redring replied, "I spoke with the manager of the business, Jack the Woodcutter."

"Then it was a waste of a journey," whispered the Anathemath, exuding a light puff of rank, deep green vapour. "We need to speak to the driving force behind the enterprise, Jack's daughter Piff, and, most of all, we need to find out what she is planning for the future."

"Not a complete waste," Baltigral whispered back. "The extra revenues will be useful, especially at a time when it is so hard to persuade any of my subjects to pay more."

Now it has to be said that one of the frustrations for the Anathemath was the limited intelligence of his clients. Of course, an essential part of the Anathemath's job was to persuade the lower orders, the poorer people, that those who ruled them were inherently superior, and therefore deserved their privileged position. But, given that most of his clients were pretty dim, it was a doubly difficult task. He not only had to convince the poor that they should respect their dull-witted masters but he also had to persuade himself to be polite to his clients, even when it was obvious they had completely lost the plot.

"Of course the money is welcome but it was hardly necessary to send the chancellor of your realm to up the rent and increase the tax. The local sheriff could have done that just as well. No, the point of sending someone of Redring's standing was to investigate this Piff, the woodcutter's daughter. We rarely have anyone in Numberland who is capable of breaking the mould…"

"What mould?" enquired Prince Baltigral, fearful that one of his prized possessions was under threat. "What mould?" he repeated, and then added, "I didn't know I had a mould," and then, after another pause, asked, "What's a mould?"

Out of the shadowy shape within the greenish cloud that was the Anathemath came a distinctly scoffing sound. "It's a figure of speech. In this instance, it means changing our world."

"You think this Piff could change our world?" choked Baltigral, now seriously alarmed. "We don't want any of that."

"I don't know whether she can change our world," sighed the Anathemath, mildly exasperated. "That was the point of sending Redring to meet her – to find out."

24

The launch of the furniture business on Piff's 18th birthday was the biggest event the Numberland forest had ever witnessed. Piff had cleared a large area in front of the woodcutter's dwelling and arranged a display of all the designs of furniture they had developed over the last three years. I say dwelling because by now the cottage had been considerably enlarged, with an upper floor added, all based on Numberlina's drawings which applied the Golden Mean. Indeed, it was now a fine house rather than a cottage; and alongside the house were separate one-storey buildings, with offices for Piff, Jack and their assistants.

Jill no longer spent her days bundling up wood, having been promoted to supervisor of the firewood bundling team but, to her chagrin, she had not been allocated an office. Piff felt that, since her stepmother had tried to exile her from the home, it was only right that she should exclude her stepmother from the office blocks.

The exhibition showed a range of rectangular tables, some of oak and others of pine. All had been constructed using the '3, 4, 5' formula to ensure the right angles were perfect. Each table had its own set of matching chairs. A variety of beds, from simple singles to elaborate bridal beds with ornately carved canopy frames, were on display. A whole section of the exhibition was devoted to wooden cupboards and cabinets and smaller items such as wooden bowls and spatulas. The foresters from every village came to the exhibition and all agreed they had never seen, or dared to hope to see, such fine furniture for people such as them.

"People like us can't have furniture like that," one of the villagers had exclaimed.

"Oh yes you can," Piff replied with a smile, as she ensured the exhibition's success by providing limitless amounts of befangle juice, slices of freshly baked crusty bread and, yes, freshly-grilled Numberland sausages, all free of charge.

25

And what a success! Almost every villager saw one or more pieces of furniture that they wanted.

In the weeks following the launch, demand for the furniture increased steadily. Each villager who bought a piece became a salesman for the company. Purchasers proudly exhibited their acquisitions to their neighbours and, in most cases, the neighbours became determined to buy a similar piece – or even a more expensive model.

Piff had planned the operation with meticulous care. Not only did the furniture suit the taste of the forester folk but it was also designed to fit the odd and often cramped accommodation provided by the typical village house. There were corner cabinets to make the best use of limited space; couches and beds with built-in storage; modular shelving to fill any otherwise unusable area.

At the end of the first year, Piff's furniture business had total sales of more than 5,000,000 pennies and a gross profit of 2,620,740 pennies. Even after tax at 60%, she ended the year with a net profit of 1,048,296 pennies. When this was added to the profits from the now static firewood business, Piff was showing a total profit for the year of 1,227,020 pennies. After paying Numberlina her 15%, some 184,053 pennies or 60 gold pieces, Piff still had 1,042,967 pennies' profit.

26

On the day after Piff's 18th birthday and the successful launch of the furniture business, Piff gave Numberlina a pleasant surprise. They were seated in a reception room in the main house when Piff, for the first time, initiated a discussion about maths. As she had seen the cottage turned into a manor house, she had been fascinated by the way in which each addition and extension had seemed to fit with the existing building. Numberlina's response, that it all ensued from applying the golden mean, simply whetted Piff's curiosity.

Suddenly, out of the blue, Piff said, "Tell me more about this magical number Phi."

"Wow!" said Numberlina. "This is another day to celebrate. Do I detect a genuine interest in maths for its own sake, not just to count money, calculate income or measure the dimensions of furniture?"

"Sorry I asked," said an irritated Piff.

"Only joking," Numberlina replied hurriedly. She was

delighted with Piff's question. "The formula for Phi is not too complicated: it's 1 plus the square root of 5, divided by 2:

$$Phi = \frac{1 + \sqrt{5}}{2}$$

or 1.61803398874989484820…"

"Don't do that," Piff interrupted. "I know you think it's clever to reel off all those numbers, but they don't mean anything. And neither does the formula. It doesn't make any sense. Why should such an important number have such a weird formula? Why the square root of 5, or the square root of anything? Why add 1? And why divide the result by 2?"

"You're absolutely right," Numberlina conceded. "It is a bit odd. But there is something in numbers that proves the Golden Mean is special. Let me show you. Here's a sequence of numbers."

0 1 1 2 3 5 8 13 21 34 55 89 144 223 377 610 987

"Can you see the rule behind the series of numbers?"

"No, I can't," said Piff, beginning to regret she had ever asked about Phi.

"Take the first two numbers and add them together," instructed Numberlina.

"0 and 1 is 1," Piff answered.

"Now take the second and third numbers and add them together."

"I see," said Piff. "1 and 1 is 2. 1 and 2 is 3. 2 and 3 is 5. 3 and 5 is 8. You just add the previous two numbers together to get the next number."

"That's the way!" said Numberlina excitedly. "*You're on a roll; so go for goal — sums are smart; some are not; but numbers always hit the spot — don't be stupid, don't be dumb, when number-crunching any sum — odd or even, all are keen to say exactly what they mean — if the digits start to fidget, crunch the numbers till they're numb — don't be dumb, be a smarty, join the party, revel with the Numerati!*" Numberlina was zipping around at speed, flying in circles and figures of eight, with the occasional loop-the-loop thrown in.

"Stop," ordered Piff. "What's the matter with you?"

"Sorry," said Numberlina. "But don't you just love it when a series of numbers comes together?"

Piff shrugged. "It's not that exciting. And, in any case, what have those numbers got to do with Phi or the Golden Mean?"

"Good question!" said Numberlina, pulling herself together and handing Piff a piece of silk with the first hundred numbers in the series printed on it. "Try dividing each number by the one that precedes it."

Piff reluctantly obeyed:

$$
\begin{aligned}
1/1 &= 1 \\
2/1 &= 2 \\
3/2 &= 1.5 \\
5/3 &= 1.666 \\
8/5 &= 1.6 \\
13/8 &= 1.625 \\
21/13 &= 1.615 \\
34/21 &= 1.619 \\
55/34 &= 1.618
\end{aligned}
$$

"Do you see what's happening?" said Numberlina excitedly. "Phi is 1.61803398... As the numbers in the series get bigger, the result of dividing each number by the one before it moves closer to Phi. If you take two numbers in the series much further down the line, like 317811 and 196418, and divide the first number by the second, the result will be 1.61803398873... or Phi to quite a number of decimal places."

"So this series of numbers is somehow connected with the Golden Mean," Piff surmised.

"Exactly," Numberlina agreed, delighted that Piff had understood.

"But why does the Golden Mean work? I mean why does 1.618 help us to make a rectangle, a picture or a building somehow look right?"

"Because the sequence of numbers appears widely in nature," Numberlina replied. "In many plants, the arrangement of seed heads and the number of petals in flowers, the growth of new shoots on plants, the spiral arrangement on pine cones, the bodies of insects, mammals, humanites and fairies, all seem to adhere to numbers in the series. These numbers are special in nature. We are all creatures of nature, so I guess the series makes us feel good."

Numberlina adopted a conspiratorial tone. "We've been discussing numbers as numbers but sometimes, if the real live numbers are becoming unruly, I make them line up in the order of one of the irrational numbers, like Pi or Phi. It's so funny. They have to run round each other to keep the sequence going – and of course there is no end; no pattern and no end. Sometimes a number appears twice or three times consecutively in the sequence so we have a convention that they have to take up position and jump the appropriate number of times to indicate they are repeating themselves." Numberlina felt the need to explain with an example. "The last time I ran the exercise with Phi, the result was hilarious."

> One took up his position before the decimal point (**1**.). He was perfectly happy, standing there on his own. As you know, he thinks he's rather special and is extremely self-centred. Six took up position in the first decimal place (1.**6**). As ever, she looked good, blue eyes, blonde wavy hair, very pretty. They made a handsome couple and were well-matched because, if One is self-centred, I have to admit Six is a little vain. Then of course One has to abandon prime position before the decimal point and nip round Six to take up the second decimal place (1.6**1**). One feels slightly discomfited because he rather liked being separated from the other numbers by a decimal point. Third decimal place goes to the rather plump and grumpy Eight (1.61**8**). Now One is sandwiched between the two girls. It's no secret the girls don't get on, so One has his work cut out stopping them from arguing. From this point, things start to degenerate. Nought wanders into the fourth decimal place (1.618**0**). He starts to ask questions. What does it all mean? Why are we performing the 'Why Phi' dance? Is there any point? Where will it all end?

> One finds Nought rather irritating. Once Nought has started to talk, he can be difficult to stop. One wants to shut him up. He says, "That's a pretty stupid question. It doesn't end. That's the whole point of an irrational number; it doesn't end – ever."

"A bit like me," says Nought. "In a way, I go on for ever."

"If you mean," says One sharply, "that you have a tendency to drivel on interminably, no one will argue with you. But if you're suggesting you have the rich and varied texture of a never-ending irrational number, let me tell you, you don't even reach the starting line, much less continue for ever."

One is beginning to feel uncomfortable between the two girls. He's tall and straight; Eight is a little rotund. One likes his own space. "Could you possibly move along a little," he suggests to Eight.

At this point Three takes up the fifth decimal place (1.6180**3**) so it's not easy for Eight to give One more room. She gives Nought a gentle shove. Unfortunately Nought catches Three in mid jump. Three is jumping to indicate he is also occupying the sixth as well as the fifth decimal place (1.61803**3**). Now Three is a rather delicate individual, a bit on the androgynous side. Bopped in mid-air by the shoved Nought, Three lands badly and falls over. Six can't resist sniping at Eight.

"That's your fault," Six shouts across One to Eight. It's not just that Six enjoys goading Eight; she's always had a soft spot for Three. "If you weren't so fat, One would have had room to breathe and there would have been no need for shoving."

"Who are you calling fat, you anorexic little trollop," retorts Eight.

Nine arrives to take the seventh decimal place (1.618033**9**). He exudes an air of authority. He helps Three to his feet. Being the square of Three, Nine has a natural affinity for his weaker brother. Three is badly shaken. His recovery is not helped by the arrival of a still angry Eight who has bundled past Nought, Three and Nine to take the eighth and ninth decimal places (1.6180339**88**). She settles into the eighth position (1.6180339**8**) and then jumps, as required, to claim the ninth position (1.618033988). Being somewhat overweight, she lands with a thump.

"Sounds like an elephant's just hit the deck," taunts Six.

"I'll give you elephants, you air-head. I'm not fat, I'm pleasantly plump. And you're not slim; you're skinny."

"Steady on," says Seven, taking up the next place (1.6180339887). He's always rather fancied Six and won't have Eight upsetting her.

"When I want your opinion," says Eight, "I'll give it to you." Eight is now really quite angry.

"I can't take any more of this," say One.

"And so it goes on," Numberlina concludes. "Great fun. In the end, Nine manages to calm everyone down and I decide to abandon the exercise anyway."

Numberlina looked to Piff for some appreciation of her narrative and numerical expertise. Piff had fallen asleep.

27

With the first year of profits from the furniture business under her belt and with both the firewood and furniture business running smoothly, Piff revealed a plan she had discussed with no one except Numberlina.

A few days after her 19th birthday, Piff took Numberlina to one side and said, "I think we are ready for the third stage."

"Are you sure?" Numberlina asked.

This was the first time Numberlina had shown any doubt. "It's a big risk," she said, "and you could lose everything. Prince Baltigral has his eye on you and on the money you are making. He will not be satisfied even with the outrageous amounts of rent and tax you are paying him. And I'm sure the Anathemath has identified you as a danger to his client which, I can tell you, is not good news."

"I know," said Piff, "but I feel ready. We have the money to invest in the project. If we don't do it, we will be rich but we will not have fulfilled my dreams."

"*Our* dreams," Numberlina corrected her. "There is much at stake but, if you believe it will work, it is possible you will succeed. As we fairies say: *'Doubt out; faith in. Never doubt that you will win'*. You know that the numbers and I will be with you to the end, whatever that end is. And if we succeed, we can all sail away into the sunset and live happily ever after."

Piff laughed. "I like that. So I'll be able to float my boat after all and, when we sail away, it will be in one of my ships built by my own people."

28

Although Piff had told no one, she had been planning the ship-building venture for two years, from the moment she was confident the furniture business was running well.

It was the logical next step. Furniture added value to the wood but ships were worth vast amounts of money. They added value to wood at a very different level. And, when built, they needed to be furnished. She had the skilled workers. She had the means to build the ships. And she had the means to equip them.

Numberlanders were by nature seafarers so, of course, they already had boats. But Piff was planning ocean-going ships that would enable whoever owned them to be masters of the seas.

She had already bought a stretch of beach on the Numberland coast on the edge of the Irish Sea and had set up all that was needed to construct the ships. Within days, she had drafted in some of her carpenters and, with the help of Nils, a ship designer she brought in from Norway, work began.

I will not trouble you with the difficulties the ship-builders faced. A ship is not a piece of furniture. It has to sail; it has to be strong; it has to be fast. It must be able to withstand the bruising of the ocean and the raging of the rain and wind. It must be able to carry passengers, freight and crew. And, if it is to be used in war, it must carry guns and munitions. They made mistakes, even with Nils of Norway to guide them and the numbers to help with all the calculations. Some of the wood was not sufficiently weathered to face the scouring of the salt seawater and, at the beginning, they underestimated the amount of wood they would need. But they worked hard and, within a year, the first ship was finished.

Piff sold the first ship to Gunnar, Earl of Cumberland, for 5 million pennies, making a gross profit of 4 million. The second year, they built two larger ships, at a gross cost of 2 million pennies each. Gunnar bought one for another 7 million pennies, making Piff a profit of 5 million; the other, she sold to Aethelstan, the Duke of Westmoreland, for 8 million, making a profit of 6 million. After paying Numberlina her commission of 2.25 million pennies or 738 gold pieces, Piff now had a profit of 12.75 million pennies. Not bad for the first two years of the ship-building enterprise!

The more astute reader will be asking: "What about the tax?" Piff used all the money from the sale of the first ship to build the next two. But surely she had to pay 60% tax? Quite right. Except she didn't, because she didn't tell the tax collector about the ship-building operation. She argued that the ship-building operation was not making a profit because she was reinvesting all the money it had made in year one into building the next two ships. So there was no profit on which to levy the 60%.

29

That's what Piff argued. But when, in a casual conversation with Aethelstan, Prince Baltigral heard about the ship-building, he was not best pleased. More accurately but not literally, he exploded with rage. Without waiting for the advice of the Anathemath, he summoned his guards and set out for the woodcutter's cottage.

Imagine his surprise when he found that the woodcutter's cottage had become a manor house, the grandest manor house in the county, and the most beautiful. As the business had progressed, Jack and his men had extended the woodcutter's cottage outwards and upwards. The original cottage, entirely remodelled, was now merely the entrance hall to the manor house. At every stage, Piff had told Numberlina the space she needed and its purpose; Numberlina produced the drawings, always adhering to the rules of the Golden Mean; and Jack and his men had done the rest. The building was now known as Woodland Manor. Not only was it a great house, it had extensive office buildings and manufacturing outhouses. It's fair to say, Baltigral was somewhat taken aback.

"Zounds!" he exclaimed, which at the time was just about the worst swear word in the Numblish language. "What the hell is going on here?"

Piff took the prince into the main reception room of the manor and offered him a cup of juice.

"I don't want befangle juice!" exclaimed Baltigral. "I want an explanation."

"Try it," Piff insisted. "It's not your usual juice. I'm calling it Begingle. I've found a way to make it more interesting."

That was an understatement. In one of the outhouses, Piff had been experimenting with fermentation and distillation of befangle juice. With the help of couple of herbs and spices, she had created a drink fit to give princes or, as Numberlina observed, if drunk to excess, a drink to give princes a fit.

Baltigral drank and, after a couple of glasses, began to mellow.

"We've made up an advertising jingle for Begingle," said Piff.

> *At a party, when you mingle*
> *and your taste buds start to tingle,*
> *whether you be wed or single,*
> *drink a glass of Piff's Begingle.*

"Look," said Baltigral, unimpressed. "I understand you've been making ships and selling them behind my back. Now you know the rules. You have to pay me – well not me, the county of Numberland – 60% of all your profits. Where's my 60%?"

"I've paid you 60% on all my profits," said Piff in feigned surprise at the prince's demand. I sent you 60% of all we made on the firewood and furniture operations. The shipbuilding hasn't made a penny yet."

"But you sold Aethelstan a ship for 8 million pennies. You're not telling me that's what it cost."

Baltigral was out of his depth. He had no idea what it cost to build a ship.

"Have another glass of Begingle," suggested Piff.

"Don't you try to befangle bejingle me," said Baltigral, but he took the offered glass anyway. "When will you make a profit? When will I get my 60%? When will you owe me what you pay me?"

"It's unlikely I will ever owe you what I pay you because if I've paid you, I won't owe you," said Piff soothingly, "but, by the end of next year, we should take another look at the situation. I'm sure then I can explain anything that's not clear."

"Clot near, clot near!" mumbled the exasperated and inebriated prince.

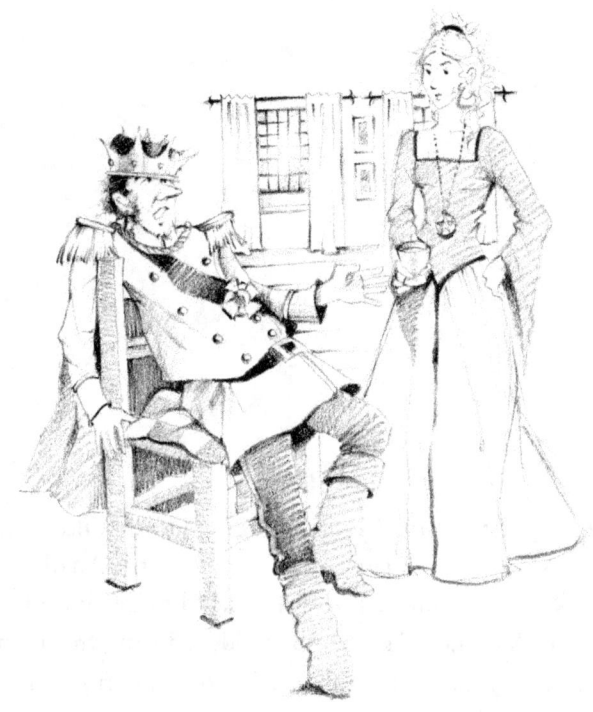

"Where?" enquired Piff, looking around.

"Where's what?" asked the prince, finishing off his third glass of Begingle.

"The nearby clot," said Piff innocently. "I'm sure you're right. But where is he?"

Baltigral shook his head, which was a mistake as the world had already started to rotate erratically. "Who cloke of spots?" he demanded. "Not I! Are you talking I somehow seriously suggest nonsense?" His words disordered and slurred, he surfed on a surfeit of sibilants.

"Of course not," said Piff. "I'm sure, when you're less begingled, you're a shining wit."

30

When Prince Baltigral returned to Old Hexam, he immediately consulted with the Anathemath. "You've no idea what they've done to the woodcutter's cottage," he complained, suffering from a mild hangover. "It's unrecognisable. It's now the finest manor house in all Numberland. It's a good deal more beautiful than this palace."

"I think it would be more useful to discuss Piff's ship-building activities," said the Anathemath, irritated, as ever, by the prince's lack of focus.

"You don't understand," Baltigral persisted. "People judge a man by his possessions. I am the prince. I should have, I must have, the finest home in the land. That Woodland Manor is a smack in the face."

Anathemath felt tempted to demonstrate to his client the difference between a distant, albeit beautifully proportioned, building and a real smack in the face but he restrained himself.

"I have seen Woodland Manor and it is indeed a fine building and I'm really sorry if it upsets you," said the Anathemath in conciliatory tones, "so why don't we explore ways of humbling the upstart, this woodcutter's daughter."

"But why is the building so fine?" Baltigral wouldn't give in. "She's not an architect; she's not a designer. I hire the best architects and designers and yet somehow she, on her own, manages to convert a cottage into a palace."

"It's not a palace; it's a manor house," said the Anathemath, "and Piff didn't design it or, if she did, she had a great deal of assistance. Now let's think of a way we can make you feel better. Let's consider if there is a way we might, for example, confiscate her manor house and indeed everything else she owns."

At last the Anathemath had succeeded in channelling Prince Baltigral's attention in a more productive direction. He had no wish to attempt to explain to the prince the Golden Mean, or indeed any of the Numerati's other magic numbers.

31

Piff, on the other hand, was eager to learn more.

One evening, on the terrace of Woodland Manor, Piff was sitting with Numberlina, reviewing the business revenues.

"We are making good money," said Piff, "and most of it is being invested in ship-building. But I notice that every day, we have quite a bit of money sloshing around in our accounts. Is there anything we could do with the spare cash?"

"There is," said Numberlina slowly, "you can put the money with Ronald Albany Softcok, the moneylender in Old Hexam. He's a Scotsman of Russian descent. Ronald will find someone who needs to borrow your money. He will charge the borrower interest, say 10% per annum, and he will give you, the lender, 2%."

"That's ridiculous," said Piff. "It's my money. Why should he make five times as much as me?"

"You have no idea," said Numberlina. "In the future, there will be organisations called banks. They will pay you

2% and lend the money to borrowers at 20% or 50% or even at 1,000%."

"But what do they do for all that money?" asked an incredulous Piff.

"Very little. Of course there's always a risk that a borrower will not pay the money back but, as you will discover if you ever borrow, the moneylender likes to take something of yours worth more than your debt as security."

"I think I'm in the wrong business," said Piff. "We have to come up with ideas; we have to develop them; we have to design products that people want; we have to make them; we have to sell them. The moneylender just takes my money, lends it to someone else and makes far more profit than I do."

"You're right," said Numberlina, "but we can't all be moneylenders. Moneylenders don't make anything. Moneylenders need people like you so that they can borrow your money to lend to other people like you."

"So what do they do with all the money they skim off?" asked Piff.

"They become very rich," Numberlina replied. "They become very greedy, always wanting more for doing less. Sometimes they become so greedy and take so much money that they ruin everyone. Indeed it's said of Ronald that he'd happily ruin the county if he could make a decent profit on it."

"That's awful," said Piff. "We won't have anything to do with them."

"I'm afraid you have to if you want to put your spare cash to work."

32

In the next year, Piff built four ships at a total cost of 8,000,000 pennies. She converted the remaining 4.25 million pennies into 1,400 gold pieces (a gold piece costing 3,035 pennies at the time) and kept this gold in reserve.

When the ships were finished and furnished, she sold them for 8 million pennies each. She now had a gross profit of 24 million pennies. After paying Numberlina her 15% (or 3.6 million pennies), she had 20.4 million pennies which she converted into gold which at the going rate gave her 6,800 gold pieces. She added this hoard of gold to the 1,400 in her reserve, so that she now had 8,200 gold pieces.

33

With so much money coming in, Piff realised she would have to put the spare cash with the moneylender. He would keep the money safe and he would pay her at least something by way of interest.

Ronald Albany Softcok, known to everyone as Ronnie, came from the lands to the north of Numberland. His company, with its distinctive symbol of a Winged Frodo, was immensely rich.

"How much money can you deposit with me and for how long?" he asked as soon as Piff had entered his office in the most expensive district of Old Hexam.

"Suggest he shows you the courtesy of providing you with a cup of befangle juice and a biscuit or two," urged Numberlina. "Make it clear you are important. He needs you at least as much as you need him."

Piff, embarrassed, hissed to Numberlina to be quiet.

"Don't worry," said Numberlina happily. "He can't see me. Indeed, he's so obsessed with money, he sees little else."

"A cup of befangle juice would be welcome," Piff hazarded.

Ronnie looked Piff up and down, estimated she could well be worth quite a lot of money and immediately called an assistant to provide both juice and biscuits.

"I could put 5,000 gold pieces with you for one year," Piff answered Ronnie's question.

"A goodly sum," conceded Ronnie, who was already working out how much he could make if he offered 2% and lent the money out as 20%. He should be able to make 900 gold pieces in one year.

"I shall expect 5% interest," said Piff who had been well-briefed by Numberlina.

"5%!" scoffed Ronnie. "I can't pay 5%."

"Get up to leave," ordered Numberlina.

"Wait, wait," Ronnie intervened hurriedly. "Let's talk about the rate. I'm sure we can come to a satisfactory compromise."

"I'm sure we can," said Piff, beginning to enjoy herself. "The compromise is 5%."

Ronnie quickly worked out that, even if he paid 5%, he would still make 750 gold pieces. Obviously, the young lady was not in a mood to bargain and he would be foolish to miss out on such a tempting profit by haggling.

"Very well," said Ronnie. "As a special introductory offer, as you're a new client, I'm prepared to give you an extraordinarily high return on your capital. 5% it is."

"You're not giving me anything. It's the other way round. I'm giving you the opportunity to use my money to make yourself rich."

Ronnie was stunned. No one talked to him like this. He wanted to tell this young woman to mind her manners but greed advised him to put up with her bluntness – and he had always found greed to be an excellent counsellor.

"Compound interest," said Piff.

Ronnie frowned. "I will pay you 5%, or 250 gold pieces, at the end of the year," he said firmly.

"No, you won't," said Piff. "You will be making money throughout the year. And so will I."

At this point, I should mention that Numberlina had explained to Piff in general terms the advantages of compound interest. If she earned 5% on her 5,000 gold pieces at the end of the year, she would receive 250 gold pieces. But if Ronnie paid interest half yearly, she would get more because, for the second six months, he would have to pay 5% on the interest she had already earned as well as on the capital. The interest after six months would be 125 gold pieces. The interest on 5,125 gold pieces over the next six months would be 128.12 gold pieces, making a total of 253.12 gold pieces (an extra 3.12 gold pieces). And, if Ronnie paid interest monthly, Piff would earn even more interest – 256.23 gold pieces (an extra 6.23 gold pieces).

According to Numberlina, Ronnie hated paying compound interest. If he paid Piff only at the end of the year, he could earn additional profit throughout the year by lending out any interest that was paid to him on short term loans that had been financed by Piff's money. In effect, he was making compound profit all the time, while those who lent him money were paid only once, at year end. Oh yes, Ronnie was full of tricks like that. Hence he could afford offices in Old Hexam's most expensive district, and much else besides.

"You will pay me the interest monthly," said Piff firmly, "or I walk."

Ronnie shrugged. He was deeply offended by Piff's dictatorial attitude but a deposit of this size was too good an opportunity to lose.

"Should I ask for interest weekly or even daily?" Piff whispered to Numberlina.

"No, it's not worth it," Numberlina replied. "Remember 'e'."

Piff had no idea what Numberlina meant but she made no further demands of Ronnie.

"Can I take it we have a deal?" said the somewhat battered Ronnie, offering his hand for a handshake.

"I'd prefer a contract," said Piff, ignoring Ronnie's offered hand.

When they had left Ronnie's office, Numberlina praised Piff. "Excellent," she said. "I'm proud of you. Sadly we need moneylenders but we should see them for what they are and treat them accordingly. They put on airs and graces but they are simply salesmen. They sell money, not their money but your money and, without adding anything of value, they aim to make ten times more profit than you do. Although moneylenders tend to be rather good at maths, the Numerati hold them in very low esteem."

Piff could see why. She had taken an instant dislike to Ronnie who seemed to be somehow arrogant and grovelling at the same time.

"What was that about 'e'?" Piff asked. She was puzzled by Numberlina's 'Remember e' remark.

"Oh, yes," Numberlina laughed. "That was silly of me. You couldn't remember 'e' because we haven't discussed it. It's another of our magical numbers. It has lots of uses, especially for woodland fairy folk but, in this case, it tells you that increasing the frequency of interest payments gives you an increased return each time but the increase is smaller each time, until, at 'e', it becomes infinitesimal."

"You've lost me," said Piff.

"Let's say you have one gold piece and you lend it to Ronnie at 100% interest for one year."

"That would be great," Piff interjected.

"Dream on," said Numberlina. "I'm saying 'one gold piece at 100%' just to make the maths easy. Now, at the end of the year, you have two gold pieces; your original gold piece and the one gold piece he must pay you in interest. But let's say you insist he pays you interest twice in the year: once after six months and once at year end. After six months he must give you interest of 0.5 of a gold piece (one gold piece divided by 2 because it's only half a year); but for the next six months, he must pay you interest on 1.5 gold pieces so he must give you 0.75 gold pieces in interest (one and a half gold pieces, divided by 2), instead of 0.5. So, you end the year with interest of 1.25 gold pieces which, when added to your original one gold piece, gives you a total of 2.25 gold pieces."

"That's quite a bit more, a quarter of a gold piece or about 750 pennies," observed Piff.

"Now if you negotiate to have your interest paid quarterly, you will earn even more interest (1.44 gold pieces) giving you a total of 2.44 gold pieces. Monthly compound interest will give you a total of 2.61 gold pieces. Weekly compound interest will give you a total of 2.69 gold pieces. Daily interest will give you a total of 2.71. Each time, the interest increases, but each time by a smaller amount. There comes a point, at 2.718…, where the increase is infinitesimal. And that is 'e'."

Piff understood the general principle. "So why didn't we ask for weekly or daily interest?"

"Not worth the bother for such a small gain," Numberlina replied. "And we don't want to appear avaricious or money-grubbing. We can leave that to greedy, seedy Ronnie. But remember that e, like Pi and Phi, is another great Numerati invention, another irrational number that defies time and space because it goes on for ever."

34

On Piff's 21st birthday, she threw a party at Woodland Manor to celebrate her success. The firewood business was still trundling along, now largely managed by Jill. The furniture business, like the firewood business, had levelled off but was running smoothly under Jack's supervision and still generating profits. Ship-building was now the biggest part of the business and obviously had the greatest potential.

And, as much by luck as by planning, there was the possibility of a fourth string to Piff's bow. Begingle.

All seemed to be well. The party was in full swing, with thousands of villagers gathered from all over the forest, enjoying Piff's hospitality.

And then Prince Baltigral arrived, with a large retinue including a dozen bodyguards together with their captain, one Tom O'Heneny, a former soldier from Ireland.

"I must be one of the few in Numberland who has not received an invitation to this splendid and costly party," said the prince.

"You are most welcome," said Piff graciously. "I did not think the birthday of one of your humble subjects would be of any interest to the Prince of Numberland but, now you are here, you, your retinue and the royal guard are my most honoured guests."

As she said these words, she noticed behind the prince a shadowy figure. She couldn't make out his precise shape or features. It seemed to be shrouded in a vague cloud of greenish haze. Piff blinked, trying to focus on the entity, but it was no use. The shape remained obscure.

"I'd rather you looked at me when I am talking to you," said Baltigral sharply.

"I'm sorry," said Piff.

"I'm here to talk to you about the tax you owe," the prince continued. "It's clear from the lavish entertainment with which you are celebrating your birthday that you are not short of a penny or two."

"Perhaps we could leave talk of tax until the party has ended," suggested Piff.

"I'm afraid we can't," snapped Baltigral. "You have yet to pay a penny on your ship-building business. Chancellor Redring reckons by now you must owe millions."

"Very well," said Piff. "Let's go to my office. We can discuss the matter there without ruining my party."

Piff, Prince Baltigral and his accompanying cloud-encased shadow-companion of greenish hue made their way to Piff's office in a building adjacent to the house. When they were settled, Piff seized the initiative.

"Your tax rates are too high. At 60% you have effectively prevented me from growing the firewood and furniture businesses. If you tax my ship-building at that rate, you will strangle the operation. I won't have the funds for development or the cash flow to build more ships. 10% of something is better than 60% of nothing."

Baltigral was confused and shocked. He didn't know what cash flow was and he certainly didn't like the sound of 10%. "You're not suggesting you pay only 10% tax? If everyone paid just 10%, the county would be bankrupt."

"I'm not sure that's true," said Piff slowly. "You yourself might go bankrupt but the county would be much the same as it is now, except that it would have much more money to spend."

Prince Baltigral was flabbergasted. What was this rude, over-confident and yet at the same time irritatingly attractive young woman saying?

"She is a danger to you," whispered the figure behind the prince. "She is questioning the way things are. You must strike now and strike hard."

"What should I say? What should I do?" asked a flummoxed Baltigral.

"Agree to 10% tax on all her businesses," said the Anathemath. "After all, that's more in line with what they charge in Cumberland and Westmoreland."

"But I'll be ruined," sobbed the prince. "How is that striking now and striking hard?"

"Agree to the 10% and then suggest we discuss the price she must pay for the wood she uses. All her products, from the firewood to the great ships, are made from the wood of the forest. And yet she pays nothing for the wood, which is your wood, taken from the forests, which are your forests, growing on the land which is your land. She will owe you so much from her businesses over the last six years that she won't even be able to pay 10% on her profits, assuming there are any profits at all, when she has paid for the wood."

Piff overheard the Anathemath's whispered advice. She responded at once. "By custom and practice, the forest belongs to all of us. From time immemorial, foresters have had the right to gather wood."

"To gather wood," hissed the Anathemath, "but not to fell whole trees, not to take the wood to make furniture, not to strip acres of land to build great ships. You have been selling a product you do not own. You have defrauded your prince. You have committed treason. Your fortune is lost; best now to concentrate on saving your life. Treason is, after all, a capital offence."

"Go back to your party," ordered Prince Baltigral. "We need to work out the price we will charge for the wood you have stolen. Tomorrow we will meet again. Tomorrow, we will tell you what you must pay and what punishment you must face for your theft and your treason. And I warn you now, the punishment for theft will be a fine at least as large as all you possess and for treason your life will be in the balance."

35

That evening when all the party-goers had left, Piff sat down in her favourite chair on the terrace and warmed herself by the brazier that she kept stocked with wood for chilly evenings.

"I told you it would come to this," said Numberlina who alighted on the arm of Piff's chair. "Now it is us against the Anathemath."

"What can we do?" Piff asked. "Baltigral can demand anything he likes for the wood."

"Not so fast," said Numberlina. "We can dispute his right to charge for the wood. Even if we agree, we can negotiate on price. But, before we do anything, you have to understand two things. First, it's all about numbers. Secondly, in the end, it will be a fight between us and the Anathemath."

"What do you mean, it's all about numbers?" asked Piff. To her, it seemed to be more about Prince Baltigral's guards and the threat of a charge of treason.

Numberlina smiled. "How many gold pieces do you have?"

"I'm not sure. I spent most of the profit on the firewood and furniture businesses on developing the ship-building operation, and on extending Woodland Manor and its outbuildings. I think I still have about 8,000 gold pieces."

"You have 8,200," said Numberlina. "And I have 2,200. Together we have 10,400 gold pieces."

"Yes, but the 2,200 are yours," Piff pointed out.

"No, they are ours," said Numberlina solemnly. "One of my three conditions for helping you was that we should stand together against the Anathemath. That is what we must now do. I have saved all my commission for this purpose. Fairies have no use for gold pieces. I took the gold to make sure we had enough when the time came. Do you realise that 10,400 gold pieces is more, much more, than Prince Baltigral can lay his hands on? Money is power and, at this moment, we have more power than him."

"But he has his guards," Piff pointed out.

"And he has to pay them," Numberlina responded. "As things stand, we would find it a good deal easier to pay them than the prince."

"But they are loyal to the prince," Piff objected.

"Of course they are," said Numberlina, "but, believe me, they are even more loyal to their wallets. In the end, it will be all about numbers."

"And what about the Anathemath? How are we to fight him?" asked Piff. "And what is the Anathemath, anyway? What does he want?"

"He is the Opposer of Progress. He is the Enemy of Education. He is the Lord of Lethargy, both physical and mental. Above all, he is the Muddler of Minds. The prince's power in Numberland depends upon the consent of the people. We have to persuade the people they would be happier with you as their princess than with Baltigral as their prince. The Anathemath will do all in his power to stop you."

"But I don't want to replace Baltigral and I certainly don't want to be a princess. That really would be treason and it's not my thing anyway," Piff objected.

Numberlina smiled. "You are the chosen one. For centuries, Numberland has been oppressed by the Baltigrals of this world. They sit in their palace in Old Hexam and they tax the people. They tax them hard and they keep them poor. And what do they do with all the tax? Well, tomorrow, I think we should find out."

Piff was shocked. She had never thought of herself as a revolutionary but, given the threats Baltigral had made, perhaps she had no choice.

"I must go now," said Numberlina. "I have much to do before morning."

36

In the morning, it was difficult to tell who was the more shocked, Piff or Prince Baltigral.

In front of the manor house, a stage had been erected and, facing it, a huge semi-circular outdoor auditorium with row upon row of tiered seating. The day was a little chilly but dry, with the sun shining down through a cloudless sky.

"What is all this?" gasped Piff, when Numberlina joined her.

"You can see what it is," said a rather out-of-breath Numberlina. "What you mean is how did it get here? The answer is simple. I built it. Not with my own hands, I hasten to add, but with the help of the numbers and a quantum of fairy magic. Before I built it, I paid a visit to an old friend of mine, Tom O'Heneny. He and I hail from the same part of Ireland and have worked together before. As I recall, the incident involved the rescue of a maiden from the clutches of a dragon vulnerable only to a sword, tipped with fairy metal. Anyway that's another story."

"You're not planning a bloody battle or an assassination?" said Piff.

"Why would I build a stage and auditorium for an assassination?" Numberlina scoffed. "No, but I am preparing for a battle, a battle of sorts. Tom has agreed to act as chairman of a debate about who should run Numberland. He will invite Baltigral and you to present your case to the people of Numberland, and then the people can decide."

"But Prince Baltigral won't agree," said Piff. "Why should he?"

"Because he will have no choice. You will insist and Tom will support you. The guards will follow Tom. He is respected and admired by his men. Oh, and just to be safe, I have promised every member of the guard the equivalent of three months' salary in gold, if they cooperate. And, I've also promised that we will continue to pay them generously if, at the end of the debate, you are the winner."

"My goodness," gasped Piff. "You seem to have thought of everything."

"Not everything," Numberlina sighed. "There is still the Anathemath. There's no doubt you could run rings round Baltigral. He's not a prince among men in anything other than name. But the Anathemath, he's an altogether different cauldron of toads. I have a feeling that, if Baltigral gets into difficulties, the Anathemath will find some way to protect him. If he does, be careful. The Anathemath, with his one eye or two eyes or no eyes for that matter, is clever and can confuse and mislead the people. And he can even find ways to frustrate the will of fairies.

37

The Great Debate, as it later became known, began at 10 o'clock in the morning when everyone had finished breakfast.

Piff had delivered her challenge to Prince Baltigral two hours earlier. At first Prince Baltigral had understandably demurred. But, when the Commander of the Guard had pointed out that a refusal would be interpreted by the masses as weakness and cowardice, he had reluctantly agreed to participate.

The Anathemath had been encouraging. "You have nothing to worry about. You are the prince. This Piff is an upstart. True, she has money, but you have every right to take her money from her. Without money, she is nothing but a nuisance."

Prince Baltigral was pleased with the Anathemath's endorsement but was still not convinced that victory would be easy or even certain.

"There are rumours circulating that she has a great deal

of support," Baltigral suggested.

"From whom?" demanded the Anathemath. "If you mean she has some support from the people, surely that does not concern you. They are the leaden, lumpen mass. They are stupid and selfish. Not that it's stupid to be selfish, I hasten to add. They just happen to be both. They find it difficult to follow an argument. In the end they will choose whoever offers them most. Just make sure it's you."

Persuaded he must participate in the debate, Prince Baltigral decided to make it a memorable, royal occasion. The royal trumpeters blasted out a fanfare to announce the opening of the event. The Royal Guard, with Tom O'Heneny at their head, marched on to the stage and stood at ease.

Tom spoke. "We are gathered here to listen to the words of Baltigral, Prince of Numberland, and Piff, the woodcutter's daughter."

Baltigral had insisted that he and Piff should be introduced in this way. He hoped that the contrast between his status as Prince of all Numberland and Piff's, as the woodcutter's daughter, an upstart of humble origin, would give him victory before either of them spoke.

"Prince Baltigral is the first to address you," said Tom.

"My people," Prince Baltigral began. He had been well-tutored by the Anathemath. "Why am I your prince? I am your prince by right of birth and blood. Like my father and his father before him, I was born to reign in Numberland. From my earliest years, I have been schooled in my responsibilities to the state and to you, my people. And I have discharged these duties with meticulous care. My rights and my responsibilities have been ordained by God. Whoever challenges me, disrespects the divine will."

Baltigral sat down. In his mind, the matter was settled.

38

Meanwhile, Numberlina had returned to her fairy dome to martial the numbers.

"The time has come," she said. "Piff is challenging Prince Baltigral. We must be ready to support her nine times, nay, ninety-nine times, nay, even should it be necessary, nine hundred and ninety-nine times."

I should explain, dear reader, that the numbers 9, 99 and 999 had a special significance for the fairies of the Numerati.

Nine, itself, was highly regarded by the other numbers. As the square of Three, which represented the union of One and Two, and as the largest of the single digit integers, Nine had a special place in the hearts of all numbers. And, amongst mankind, Nine was generally considered a lucky number.

We should also note that Nine has a special affinity with One, perhaps because they mark the first and the last of the integer range. Nine together with One, has always been able to engender a high degree of harmony amongst all the numbers. Indeed, if you divide 111,111,111 by 9, the result will be 12,345,679. (Eight, being a little over-weight, arrived too late to join the party, as Numberlina would often remark.)

Integer	Divisors				Totals
1	1				1
2	1	2			3
3	1	3			4
4	1	2	4		7
5	1	5			6
6	1	2	3	6	12
7	1	7			8
8	1	2	4	8	15
9	1	3	9		13
10	1	2	5	10	18
11	1	11			12
Total					99

99, composed of two Nines, was again considered of special quality. 99 is the sum of the cubes of Two, Three and Four ($2^3 + 3^3 + 4^3 = 99$) and the sum of the divisors of the first 11 positive integers.

99 is also a number whose square (9801) can be divided into two parts (98 and 01) which, when added together, equal itself (99). This is a further example of the special affinity of Nine with One.

As for 999, it was regarded by the Numerati as one of the most powerful of all numbers. A palindromic number, the sum of its constituents (9 + 9 + 9) 27, when added together (2 + 7) gives 9 and when multiplied by the prime number 37 (27 x 37) equals 999. The square of 999 (998001), like the square of 99, can be divided into two parts (998 and

001) which, when added together, gives 999. And 999, the inverted form of 666 (the number of the beast), is the closest any combination of numbers can approach to the God of the Numerati.

Hence Numberlina's invoking of the numbers 9, 99 and 999.

While Numberlina was exhorting the numbers to prepare themselves for battle and the male numbers in particular were competing with each other with vows of future valour, no one noticed the faint, greenish haze that had infiltrated the fairy dome and which had settled quietly, close to the ground, listening to all that was said.

39

Back at Woodland Manor, it was Piff's turn to respond to Prince Baltigral's opening salvo.

"Friends," Piff began, "friends and fellow workers."

Baltigral fidgeted uneasily. That was clever. He had adopted the role of father to his people whereas Piff was treating them as equals, using 'fellow-workers' to emphasise how much they had in common.

"Prince Baltigral bases his right to rule us and tax us on claims of birth and blood. But we know the history of Numberland. The Baltigral family were not always the rulers of our county. Four generations back, the prince's great-great-grandfather seized the throne by the simple expedient of murdering the then Prince Amenon and marrying his widow. Sounds to me more like the divine right of might, rather than God's will."

There was a murmur in the audience made up of shocked surprise at Piff's audacity, mixed with admiration for her courage.

Prince Baltigral rose to speak and Piff gave way.

"I do not base my claims to your allegiance solely on my right of birth, although I would point out that, by blood, no one has a better claim to Numberland's throne than I. No, I also base my claim on merit. As I think I mentioned, throughout my early years, I was tutored in the skills required to rule this land. I number amongst my friends, the princes of the neighbouring counties, Gunnar, Earl of Cumberland and Aethelstan, Duke of Westmoreland. Each of us knows our duty to our counties and the people. For the last ten years, there has been peace throughout these lands. As a result, you, the people, have prospered. No parent has had to bury their child, killed in battle. Those with initiative, amongst whom I count this woodcutter's daughter, have been able to build businesses. As a result of my good governance, there have been sufficient Numberland sausages and loaves of bread and jugs of befangle juice for all."

Prince Baltigral resumed his seat to a loud round of applause from the audience. He felt a little sorry for Piff. This was going to be embarrassing. It would be best for her if she politely conceded defeat and withdrew.

"I cannot claim to be friends with Gunnar, Earl of Cumberland, or Aethelstan, Duke of Westmoreland. But I have done business with both. As many of you know, they bought my first ships. The prince talks much of his good governance and I agree that war is a disaster and life is better for all in times of peace. But all the benefits that have ensued from peace came from the wit of those who set up businesses and the honest labour of the people who helped to make their businesses succeed.

"The time has come to talk numbers," Piff continued, now hitting her stride. "Of course we need leadership. But we pay for that leadership with our taxes. It is therefore reasonable to ask:

How much do we pay?
What do we get for what we pay?
Is what we get good value for money?

"I think the answers will be 'too much, too little and no'."

Prince Baltigral was on his feet. "Such questions go beyond the remit of this discussion. You encroach on county secrets; on matters, which for reasons of policy, must remain confidential. To reveal such information would put our security in grave peril."

It was such an authoritative intervention that most, if not all, in the audience seemed satisfied. Until Piff asked a one word question: "Why?"

Baltigral spluttered for a moment and then replied. "I just told you why. These are county secrets which, if revealed, would jeopardise our security."

"How does publication of the county's revenue and expenditure figures jeopardise our security? Unless you have something to hide and it's your own security that could be at risk."

This was a frontal attack on the prince. "Treason!" exclaimed the prince. He turned to the Commander of the Guard.

Tom O'Heneny shook his head. "We should hear what she has to say," he whispered in Baltigral's ear. The words sounded like helpful advice but Baltigral was smart enough to know he must tread carefully. He made a mental note to deal with O'Heneny at a later date on a less public occasion.

"Explain yourself," said Baltigral to Piff.

"I would have preferred to discuss the royal accounts," said Piff. "But, if you refuse to reveal your revenue and expenditure, I will simply ask the audience to consider my own contribution to your coffers. You have set the tax on my profits at 60%. For every 100 pennies I make, you take 60p. In the last three years on the firewood and furniture business, I have made 7.3 million pennies and I have paid you 4.7 million pennies in tax. I have estimated on the most generous assumptions, your total expenses including your administration, all your staff, the costs of Old Hexam Palace, the maintenance of all your property and your personal guard and it comes to less than I have paid in tax. And I am just one of the businesses in Numberland. With the help of my employees, I have been successful, but there are others in Numberland who have also enjoyed success. Let's say I contribute one third of your total revenues. I must then ask you what you have done with what I estimate should be about 9 million pennies or 3,000 gold coins."

Prince Baltigral was now beginning to regret withholding his accounts. Piff's estimates grossly exaggerated his financial good health. She had omitted the vast sums he had to spend on bribery (to dissuade any rivals for power from conspiring against him) and the money he paid regularly to town and village headmen (to make sure they kept the people quiet). Where was the Anathemath when you needed him?

40

When the Anathemath had heard enough of the numbers' preparations for battle, he began to adopt a more defined shape within the fairy dome, rising from the green mist, close to the forest floor, up into a distinct cloud with the blurred figure of a man at its centre.

"I tell you what," he said.

Every one of the numbers started and shuddered. Numberlina fell off the branch where she had been standing to address the numbers and had to activate her wings in a hurry to avoid hitting the ground.

"You all think you are so brave and so clever," the Anathemath continued, "so I'll give you a puzzle, a puzzle with numbers. See if you can find the answer. If you succeed, good for you. If, on the other hand, you fail, the omens for your chosen one, this Piff, the woodcutter's daughter, will be poor indeed."

The Anathemath did not wait for a response. He knew

that the numbers would not be able to resist a seemingly simple mathematical problem and would be deeply disconcerted if they were unable to find a solution. In this way, he would soften them up for the final test he would use to break them.

> "Three travelling companions rent a room in an inn for the night. On arrival they pay 30p (10p each) and go to their room.
>
> A little later the innkeeper's daughter, a buxom wench, brings up a flagon of beer and gives the companions back 5p. The inn is celebrating its 10th anniversary and is giving a special discount that weekend. Out of the 5p rebate, the three companions decide to each keep 1p and give the innkeeper's daughter a rather generous 2p tip.
>
> When, the following morning, the companions sit down to reconcile their expenses, they find they cannot make sense of the figures. Each one of them had originally paid 10p. Then each got back 1p which meant that they each paid 9p. So, together, they had paid 27p. They had given the innkeeper's daughter 2p, which accounted for 29p. What happened to the other 1p?"

The Anathemath knew that the numbers found any riddle involving maths tempting and, if they failed to find a solution, deeply frustrating. What better way to occupy and waste their time, while undermining their self-confidence?

Numberlina intervened immediately. "We have no time to play games with you. Shouldn't you be helping your client at

Piff's manor? Without your help, he is likely to find himself up the creek and out of his depth."

But her intervention was too late. The numbers were already wrestling with the Anathemath's seemingly simple riddle.

41

Numberlina was right.

Piff's estimate of Prince Baltigral's income and expenditure had shocked the people in the audience. If Piff's figures were halfway right, the prince was taking too much and giving too little. Obviously, they didn't know about the massive amount of bribery on which Baltigral depended to keep everyone in line.

Piff waited for Baltigral to respond.

Baltigral played his last card – fear. He appealed directly to the audience. "Do you have any idea what will happen if law and order break down? I provide you all with security. You are able to lead your lives, to breed and feed, to eat your Numberland sausages and your bread, and drink your befangle juice, knowing that you will be as safe tomorrow as you are today. I give you peace and stability. This upstart offers you uncertainty and chaos. Let's be done with this. Piff, you will pay your tax or you will be a guest in my dungeon. You, my people, will go home."

It was a brave attempt but no one moved.

Then Piff stood up and said, "I want to tell you a story. It's about me and my family. You all know I am the woodcutter's daughter. Some years ago, Jill, my stepmother, threw me out of my home. In those days, she was lazy, gluttonous and fat. My father and I worked but Jill did nothing but eat, drink and complain. So two of us were supporting three of us.

"I made a friend who helped me to see a way to make thing better. She told me there are two kinds of people. There are those to whom life happens; and there are those who make life happen. I decided to return home to make some changes. I started to develop the firewood business. I put my stepmother to work. Soon, there were three of us instead of two of us contributing to the household income. Things were better. Then we were able to expand the firewood business. Later we developed the furniture business. Now we are in the ship-building business. My father and stepmother work hard and have responsible, well-rewarded jobs. And I work hard. You know that. And you work hard."

That last remark generated some laughter and much applause.

Piff continued. "I'm telling you this story because it seems to me we have another case where two are working hard to support a third. My family and I work hard to develop and manage our businesses; and you, the people, work hard to enable the businesses to succeed. But what exactly does our prince do? He won't show us his accounts but I think we all know enough to conclude he's not really pulling his weight. He talks about law, order and stability and he's right, there's nothing more important to us as people and to me as a businessperson. So, if I'm your leader, you can be sure I will maintain safety and security even more keenly than the prince. And I will open my accounts to you. You will see how much you pay in tax and what the money is spent on."

There was a murmur of approval which grew into a roar.

Tom O'Heneney called for silence. "It was agreed with the contenders before the debate that, when they had had their say, you should take the rest of the day to consider the two offers. Tomorrow, we will hold a vote."

42

Back in the fairy dome, the Anathemath was smiling. Obviously, he was amused by Numberlina's suggestion he should be helping Prince Baltigral.

"You fairies are so delightfully naïve. It is in my interests that Baltigral should find himself in difficulties. Then, when, in the nick of time, I rescue him, he will be so much more grateful. Now, if you didn't like my first riddle, I will give you another. And I suggest you try to tackle this one. Why? Because my third challenge which I will insist you accept will determine the fate of Numberland. And, as I see it, you need some practise on the riddle-solving front."

> "I set before you on a table three identical boxes. In each box, there is a bar of metal. In two boxes, the bar is lead; in the third box, the bar is gold. I know which box contains the gold bar; you have no idea but would of course like to have the gold bar. I invite you to choose a box and promise you that

you can keep its contents. You choose a box but do not look inside it.

There are now two remaining boxes. If you have already chosen the box with the gold bar, both these boxes contain lead. If you have chosen a box with lead in it, one of the remaining boxes contains the gold bar; the other lead.

I now open one of the two unchosen two boxes, the one that I know contains lead. I show you the lead and discard it. There are now only two boxes left; the one you chose and one of the ones you didn't.

At this point, I ask you whether or not you would like to change your choice of box. What should you do?"

Numberlina knew the game that the Anathemath was playing. He was trying to distract her and the numbers and to undermine their confidence. The next day, the fate of Numberland would be decided. Piff would face Baltigral. Numberlina would support Piff whatever the cost and she was certain she could count on the numbers in every sense; but the numbers would not be at their best if they had spent any time wrestling with the Anathemath's riddles and failing to solve them. And Baltigral would have the full support of the Anathemath, knowing the confidence of the numbers had been thoroughly shaken. Only a fool would underestimate the Anathemath.

"We have better things to do than wrestle with your riddles or ponder your puzzles," Numberlina declared firmly.

"I'll give you a clue," said the Anathemath, ignoring

Numberlina's words. "Although it seems like a 50/50 chance that either of the two remaining boxes contains the gold bar, it's generally agreed by the greatest mathematicians that you should change your choice of box. But why? I foresee that, far in the future, there will be a game show which will feature this puzzle and cause much controversy amongst the public and even amongst professors of mathematics. But surely you, the representatives of the Numerati, can find the answer?"

It was clear to Numberlina that the Anathemath's strategy was having some effect. Several of the numbers were organising themselves in an attempt to solve one or other of the Anathemath's conundrums. And, truth to tell, they were not having much success. Even Numberlina was left wondering what on earth a game show might be.

43

That evening, Piff was having dinner with Jack and Jill in Woodland Manor when a surprise visitor arrived. It was Prince Baltigral, wearing his best suit of clothes. He was unaccompanied.

Piff made the prince welcome but came straight to the point. "Why are you here?"

The prince was clearly embarrassed. "It's a little difficult in front of your parents," he began.

"You can have nothing to say to me that my parents shouldn't hear," Piff responded.

"Very well," said Prince Baltigral, pulling himself together. "It may well be best they hear what I have to say so that we can get on with things."

"Get on with what things?" asked Piff, intrigued and alarmed in equal measure.

"I have come to ask for your hand in marriage," said the prince.

Piff was still a very young woman but she had spent years

building a business, managing people, fulfilling objectives. She had the experience of a person ten, perhaps twenty, years older. But the prince's proposal left her momentarily speechless.

The prince took the silence for grateful acceptance, assuming that Piff's joy had taken her breath away. "We can announce the betrothal tomorrow morning," he added.

"Why exactly," asked Piff, recovering the power of speech, "why exactly would I want to marry you?"

"Don't you see?" said the prince, somewhat stunned. "It will resolve all this nastiness. No need for votes, arrests and dungeons. I won't have to tax you because all your wealth will become mine, well no, not mine, ours. I shall allow you to continue working. Indeed I shall encourage it. I can foresee a happy and prosperous future for Numberland, if you and I are wed. And, I might add, if this is not inappropriate, that, for a woodcutter's daughter, you are not entirely unattractive."

Piff paused before replying. Over the years, she had learned to control her temper.

"I can see the benefits to you of the proposed marriage," she began, "but could you list the advantages to me? You seem to be suggesting I hand over to you all my wealth, both what I have and what in future I may generate, and then continue working, in effect, for nothing."

"Well, really," said the prince, deeply offended. "I am offering myself in marriage. You will become Princess of Numberland. You will live in Old Hexam Palace – that is when you're not out and about, running your businesses."

"But why should I marry a man I don't know and don't like?" asked Piff bluntly.

Prince Baltigral was now angry. "You peasants! You just don't know how to behave. I must have been mad to consider it."

"Better a rude peasant than a mad prince," Piff quipped, as Baltigral stormed out.

When the prince had gone, Jill was the first to speak. "Don't you think you were a little hasty to reject Prince Baltigral's offer out of hand? After all, you would be Princess of Numberland."

"Shut it!" was all Piff said.

44

In the morning the gathering at Woodland Manor was perhaps the greatest assembly that Numberland had ever seen. The ranks of those who had been present at the debate were now swelled by villagers and townsfolk from near and far who had heard there was to be a vote on the future of the county. There was real excitement that the people would have a say in the future of Numberland and that there might be the chance of a change for the better.

It was generally agreed that Piff had had outperformed the prince in the previous day's debate but fear of the unknown still persuaded many to support Prince Baltigral.

"The vote will be close," said Baltigral to the Anathemath who had now joined his client.

"Your cause will not have been helped by widespread rumours of your idiotic escapade last night," snapped the Anathemath.

"I don't see how my proposal to Piff was idiotic," said a subdued Baltigral.

"Well, apart from the fact that you gave her the opportunity to humiliate you, that you showed weakness, if not desperation, in your dealings with the enemy and that you failed to come up with any reason why she should accept your offer, your approach to Piff was entirely well-judged."

"I don't like sarcasm," retorted the prince. "Just remember I pay you wages."

"Well, there's another problem," said the Anathemath, unabashed but irritated. "I am renowned as a master of sarcasm; yet you employ me. You don't hire a dog and then complain when it barks. If you do, don't be surprised if the dog also bites."

"What are we going to do?" said the prince, eager to turn the conversation into a more constructive direction.

The Anathemath decided to summarise the situation. "Piff won yesterday's debate and she has the committed support of Numberlina and the numbers."

"What are you talking about?" asked the prince. "Who the hell is Numberlina? And what numbers? Numbers of what?"

I should perhaps explain that Prince Baltigral was as ignorant of the fairy folk, the numbers and the Numerati as he was of how to run a business or understand the royal accounts. That was one reason why he was so opposed to change. He had no idea how the present system worked but he knew that, from his point of view, it did. So best to leave everything alone.

"Never mind," the Anathemath continued. "Suffice it to say, there are forces backing Piff which I shall have to neutralise. I can spread fear amongst the people. I can muddle their heads with statistics so distorted that they break every rule of mathematical integrity but, unless I can neutralise those forces who want Piff to succeed, you will lose."

"What do you need to do the neutralising?" asked Prince Baltigral, eagerly. "I can put my personal guard at your disposal."

"I doubt that," said the Anathemath. "You must have noticed some recent reticence amongst the guard when you have sought their help. In any case, this is a battle I must fight alone and one I must fight on the enemy's terms. This is Numberland and I must take on Numberlina and all her numbers and defeat them, playing by her rules. Only then can I stop her from aiding Piff. It is a mighty task which, if successfully completed, is worthy of a truly mighty fee."

The Anathemath paused, waiting expectantly.

"Yes, of course," said the desperate prince. "Whatever you want. Just make sure that the arrogant little peasant person gets her comeuppance, that we collect the tax and that I remain prince."

The Anathemath smiled. This battle was now between him and Piff. To the victor, the spoils. Poor Prince Baltigral was not in it: he had already lost.

When Prince Baltigral had departed, the Anathemath settled into a more relaxed position, cosseted within his noxious green penumbra, and began to make his plans. Piff on her own was a worthy adversary but Piff, backed by Numberlina and the numbers, was even more of a problem. She was a serious challenge and a threat. He must plan carefully, undermining the opposition, step by step. He knew each of the numbers, their strengths and their weaknesses. Working together, they were incredibly powerful, but on their own they were nothing but single digits. They needed Numberlina and the power of the Numerati to reach their full potential. If he could undermine the numbers, if he could shake their confidence, then he would weaken Numberlina and could drain Piff's strength.

45

Numberlina and the numbers had set up camp in one of the unused outbuildings in the grounds of Woodland Manor. There was a spirit of cautious optimism in the group. The odd numbers, being male, tended to be more aggressive and assertive, making extravagant boasts about their prowess and the heroic feats they intended to perform. The even numbers, while no less determined to support Piff, were a little more cautious.

"We have examined Piff's arguments, as presented by her yesterday, and she has a first class case. All her figures add up," said One.

"I second that," said Two, keen to speak out on behalf of the even numbers.

"As do I," said Eight, who, being 2 cubed, had a natural affinity with Two and was eager to show her support for her fellow female even number.

"I don't mean to be picky," said the slim Six who enjoyed goading the plumper Eight, "but I've always thought, if someone has already seconded a motion, the next person to voice support is 'thirding' it."

The pale Three, with his soft skin and gentle eyes, took the opportunity to intervene before Eight could hit back. Disharmony upset him and, being the sum of 1 and 2, was delighted to see them supporting each other. "We can all agree with One and Two. As things stand Piff has an excellent chance of winning."

"Absolutely," said another even number, who, like Eight was a little on the plump side. "All the even numbers will stand together, four square with Two." Four was gratified by a round of applause from all the females and even some grunts of approval from the odd numbers.

"I'm confident we can give Prince Baltigral a good thrashing," said Seven.

"If you have the help of the even number who has her rightful place between us, I agree," said Five. "You should then have the enemy at 6s and 7s in no time."

"It's difficult to see what you can do in 'no time'," mused Nought, "given that everything takes at least a little bit of time to happen in. Still, 'nothing ventured', as I often say."

"I'm perfectly capable of dealing with Prince Baltigral on my own, without Seven's help," said Six, always a little wary of being too closely associated with the womanising Seven. "After all, without any help, I could always knock him for 6."

"Or we could get him drunk on Begingle," said Seven. "Then Nine could run rings round him."

"How do you reckon that?" enquired Nought, alerted by the mention of rings which he took to be an oblique reference to himself.

"Well, if he was inebriated, he'd be one over the eight, and therefore nicely set up for Nine."

This sally from Seven elicited a groan from several of the other numbers and an indignant rebuke from One who disliked any attempt to associate him with any particular number and, in any case, considered Eight far beneath him.

The numbers chatted on in this vein for some time. Only Numberlina and Nine said nothing. They were waiting.

"He is coming," said Nine.

Beneath the locked doors of the numbers' outbuilding a noxious green smoke was seeping. It crept across the floor and gradually mounted upwards until it looked like a large green igloo, composed of smoke, gases and something vague yet powerfully conscious at its centre.

"Good morning, Numberlina. Good morning, numbers," said a seemingly affable voice from within the vaporous greenish igloo. "I hope we can resolve this matter in a civilised manner."

"As things stand, that seems unlikely," said Numberlina. She knew of the Anathemath's tricks and was determined to be wary.

"Look, we can either fight it out, trading blows, cutting and slashing, until there is total chaos, with your numbers depleted and me, at the least, discomfited. That way, both sides will suffer damage and the outcome will be uncertain. Or we can find another way."

"And what is your other way?" Numberlina asked.

"A simple test of wits," said the Anathemath in his most emollient voice.

"What then?" Numberlina probed.

"I suggest a mathematical problem, a simple mathematical problem, one which will involve all your numbers. If you can solve the problem in one hour, I will agree to withdraw from the contest between Prince Baltigral and young Piff and leave the prince to face the vote alone. If you fail, you must agree to abandon Piff to me and to her fate. I shall be free to spread confusion amongst the masses and, as ever, they will vote for what they know, fearful of the risks of something new."

"You swear the problem will be pure maths?" Numberlina needed to be sure. If it was pure maths, surely the Numerati could solve it. As a last resort, she could always seek the help of the High Council of the Numerati. There was no mathematical problem they could not solve.

"I swear," said the Anathemath, using his most serious voice.

"And you swear you will not interfere in the struggle between Piff and Baltigral if we succeed?" Numberlina persisted.

"I swear," said the Anathemath.

"And do you swear to keep your word?" asked Numberlina.

The Anathemath laughed. "Have you forgotten the story of the Cretan liar? What does it mean if I say: 'This sentence is false'. If the sentence is true, the sentence is false. If the sentence is false, it is true. If I have sworn, you must either believe me or not. Asking me to swear that I will keep my word is pointless."

Numberlina shook her head. "There you go again, with your riddles and paradoxes. You muddle to befuddle."

"Very well," said the Anathemath, "I swear that I swear the truth when I swear I am telling the truth. But, if you want a more certain guarantee, I will put my life in the hands of the Numerati, my enemies. Long ago, the High Council of Numerati promised not to destroy me. They told me that my work, although damaging to mankind in general, was a powerful stimulus to make some men, not many mind you but a few, think and think hard. For that, they let me live. If I break my word, I release them from that promise and, if they so wish, my life will be forfeit."

"Then I agree," said Numberlina.

"Excellent," said the Anathemath. "Here, then, is the problem. The hour will begin from the moment I leave you. All I want you to do is arrange the numbers 1 to 9 into three groups of three. Each group of three must be a prime number. Obviously, you must use all the numbers but each number only once."

"Is that it?" asked Numberlina. It might take a little time but she was sure the problem could not be too difficult.

"There is one more condition," the Anathemath answered. "It's a very minor addition. I would like written solutions to those two riddles I posed earlier, you know, the three travellers at the inn and the boxes containing lead or gold."

"That's not fair," said Numberlina. "I asked if the problem we had to solve was mathematical and you said yes. You can't add in riddles."

The Anathemath sighed. "What a pity. I thought we had an agreement. Surely you can handle a couple of simple riddles. In any case, the solutions to both are based on maths. So I'm not really breaking our agreement. But if you really can't solve them…" He tailed off, allowing the smile on his face to morph into a sneer.

Everything told Numberlina not to agree but the Anathemath's sneer, in so far as she could see it within the fetid green penumbra, pushed her over the edge.

"Is that it?" she asked.

"Not quite," said the Anathemath. "I almost forgot to mention it. I know that the number 999 holds a special place in the hearts of the Numerati so, when your little band of numbers has organised themselves into three prime numbers, each consisting of three digits, the three prime numbers added together must total 999 because I know how important the number 999 is to you and all the Numerati."

Numberlina gulped. This was not going to be as easy as she had thought.

"And one final thing…" the Anathemath continued.

At this point, Numberlina could see the grinning face of the Anathemath. In the middle of his face, there was a single eye. It winked.

The Anathemath repeated, "One final thing. The High Council of the Numerati have agreed that, even if you ask them, even if you beg them, they will not give you the answer. This is between you and me. Do you see? Between just you and me."

"Oh!" said Numberlina.

46

There was a carnival atmosphere in the crowd of Numberland subjects as they waited for their first ever opportunity to vote on the future of their county.

Piff had her supporters, mainly amongst those who worked for her in the firewood, furniture or ship-building businesses. They knew she was a brilliant innovator and organiser; they respected her as their leader; and, above all, they knew she was honest and fair. Her supporters talked enthusiastically about her merits to others and they won many converts.

At the same time many, and perhaps most, tended to favour the existing arrangements. They knew their prince was greedy and lazy but he was not tyrannical and, so long as they could live their lives in peace, they saw no need to risk a change. This view was fostered, nurtured and encouraged by the Anathemath who used the hour while the numbers were wrestling with the riddles and their prime number problem to bolster support for his client. He was here, there and everywhere, whispering "Piff's too young to lead you" "Surely you don't want to be led by a woman?" "If it ain't broke, don't fix it".

When the Anathemath reported to his client, he found Prince Baltigral in a better mood. The prince's spies had reported to him that opinion seemed to be swinging in his favour.

"It's looking good," he said to the Anathemath. "Thank goodness, my people are seeing sense. I'm surprised at the change in mood, pleased of course – but surprised."

"There are two reasons why things are swinging your way," the Anathemath explained. "First, I have spent the last hour amongst your people, instilling fear of change in their hearts. They do not love you but they now fear what might follow if they oust you. Secondly, the forces ranged against you are so busy trying to solve a little problem I gave them that they have not had time to persuade the people to support Piff. You will notice both explanations have something in common. They both must be credited to me, a fact which, as we have agreed, will subsequently be reflected in my fee."

47

While the Anathemath was systematically undermining support for Piff amongst the population of Numberland, Numberlina and the numbers were desperately scrambling around trying to solve the prime number problem but their confidence had been shaken by their continuing failure to solve the Anathemath's two riddles.

They knew well enough how to construct any of the 143 three-digit primes. The first challenge was to make sure all nine numbers were used in compiling the sets of three. That proved to be relatively easy. They produced many sets of three-digit primes which employed all the numbers from 1 to 9.

127, 463, 859
149, 263, 857
263, 857, 941
281, 359, 467
281, 467, 953

281, 647, 953
359, 467, 821
359, 647, 821
479, 521, 683
647, 821, 953

But none of them totalled 999. None of them even came close.

127 + 463 + 859 = 1,449
149 + 263 + 857 = 1,269
263 + 857 + 941 = 2,061
281 + 359 + 467 = 1,107
281 + 467 + 953 = 1,701
281 + 647 + 953 = 1,881
359 + 467 + 821 = 1,647
359 + 647 + 821 = 1,827
479 + 521 + 683 = 1,683
647 + 821 + 953 = 2,421

Numberlina was beginning to panic. There were only fifteen minutes before the end of the allotted hour.

At very close to the speed of light, Numberlina left the outbuilding heading for the Council Chambers of the Numerati, housed far to the south, in Castle Integer. The Anathemath had told her that the High Council would not give her the answer but perhaps they could give a little help.

Numberlina made her way to the office of the Council's current president, the hyper-intelligent Martha Viola Fomes. Martha, who was well aware of the task that the Anathemath had set, agreed to see Numberlina immediately.

"We are having a real problem," gasped Numberlina, "and time is running out."

"I'm sorry, but we agreed with the Anathemath that we would not give you the answer," said Martha. "If you doubted your ability, you should not have agreed to the test."

"But he didn't tell me about your agreement not to help until after I had accepted his challenge," said Numberlina, now close to tears, realising that the Anathemath had tricked her.

Martha gently patted Numberlina on the head. "All is not lost. If you go to the Ancient Library of the Numerati and consult the third volume of the Book of Riddles, you will find the two riddles you need to solve, together with the solutions. We are not giving you the answers but you, like every fairy member of the Numerati, have access to the Library whenever you so wish. Return when your research is completed."

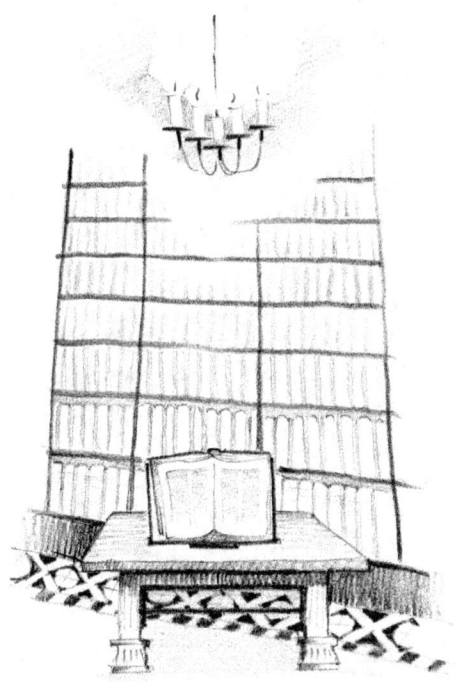

Numberlina was in the Library almost before Martha had finished speaking. There, on the main desk, open at the right page, was the third volume of the Book of Riddles. Lying on top of the page was a copy of the answers to the two riddles the Anathemath had posed. Numberlina folded the sheet carefully and slipped it into her pocket.

Martha was waiting for Numberlina. "I hope you found what you wanted," she said with a radiant smile. "Now, as for the prime number problem, again we promised not to give you the answer, and we won't. But we were most careful not to promise not to help. So I'm going to tell you a story and you must make of it what you will.

"Long ago, at the annual Numberland Games, there was intense competition in the Numberland sausage-eating contest. The audience placed their bets on the number of sausages the finalists could eat in a minute. The highest number on which anyone could bet was nine but no one had ever eaten even half that many. When all the bets were in, most bets were for lower numbers but there was one for nine. The final began with a bang. Not inappropriate for a sausage-eating contest. After much munching, there was a dead heat of several contestants. Five ate seven, a new Numberland sausage-eating record."

Numberlina frowned. And then she smiled.

The allotted time had almost elapsed. She flew back to Woodland Manor even faster than she had flown away. She had one minute left.

48

"Well," said the gloating Anathemath to an out of breath and untypically dishevelled Numberlina. "It's time for the reckoning. Do you have an answer? Or has my challenge clipped your wings, so to speak?"

"I think I have solutions to your riddles," said Numberlina.

"Really?" The Anathemath was surprised and sceptical. "Let me see."

Numberlina took out the paper she had so carefully folded and opened it.

"Read it," ordered the Anathemath.

Numberlina started with the riddle of the three travellers at the inn. She read:

> "There is no missing 1p. The three travellers pay 30p (10p each) for the room. The innkeeper's daughter reduces the 30p to 25p, when she refunds 5p so 25p is the amount paid for the room rental. She gives 1p to each traveller (total 3p) and keeps 2p for herself.

> The correct calculation is 30p − 3p − 2p = 25p. 25p is the true amount (30p − 5p) that the travellers have paid to the innkeeper for the room. Each traveller has therefore paid 8⅓p (one third of 25p) for the room and has given ⅔p (one third of 2p) to the innkeeper's daughter (i.e. each traveller has spent 9p). That accounts for 27p. The travellers originally handed over 30p but they each took a 1p rebate which brings their expenditure down to 27p. Thus all the money is accounted for (27p + 3p = 30p).
>
> The confusion arises when the 2p given to the innkeeper's daughter is added to the 27p paid by the travellers. The 27p includes the gift to the innkeeper's daughter. The room rental was 25p, not 30p. The 3p difference between 27p and 30p is the rebate, not the gift to the buxom wench."

A puff of green smoke detached itself from the penumbra of the Anathemath and diffused into the air. Although still confident he would be the victor, he was not at all happy. "What about the boxes with lead or gold bars?" he snapped.

"This one involves a diagram," Numberlina explained.

"Read your answer anyway," growled the Anathemath.

Again Numberlina read from the paper she had found in the Numerati Library.

> "Given there are only two boxes left, it would seem to be a 50:50 chance that either box contains the gold bar. And yet, although it is completely counter-intuitive, it can be shown that the best course of action is to change the box you originally chose for the other one. The chances that you

chose the correct box is only 33%. The chance that the other box contains the gold bar is 66%.

At the start, the gold bar must be in Box 1 or Box 2 or Box 3. There are therefore three possible scenarios.

Let's assume your choice was Box 1.

If you stick with your choice, there are three possible scenarios. In scenario 1, you win because you have already chosen the box with the gold bar; but in scenarios 2 and 3 (where your original choice was lead), you lose because, in either case, the gold bar must be in the one remaining box and you will lose. (Remember that, of the two you didn't choose, the riddle master removed the one that contained lead.)

If you decide to switch, again there are three possible scenarios. In scenario 1 (where you correctly chose the box containing the gold bar), you will lose; but in scenarios 2 and 3, you will win, because the gold bar must be in the one remaining box. (Again remember that, of the two you didn't choose, the riddle master removed the one that contained lead.)

	Scenario	Box 1	Box 2	Box 3	Outcome
	1	**Gold**	Lead	Lead	You win
You stick	2	Lead	**Gold**	Lead	You lose
	3	Lead	Lead	**Gold**	You lose
	1	**Gold**	Lead	Lead	You lose
You switch	2	Lead	**Gold**	Lead	You win
	3	Lead	Lead	**Gold**	You win

So you should switch."

"That's not at all clear," said the Anathemath.

"The diagram makes it clear," said Numberlina.

The Anathemath was now far from pleased. Another puff of green vapour broke away from the Anathemath. "None of this is important," declared the Anathemath. "I don't know why I included the riddles. The real test is all about the prime numbers. Have you an answer? If not, you lose."

Numberlina stood amongst the numbers. They were amazed that she had solved the riddles but were fearful she had spent too much time unravelling riddles and not enough on the main question.

"All I can do is try," Numberlina replied. "I will start with One. One is, after all, the first number. One, step forward." One obeyed immediately. He loved to be first; it just felt right. Of course others would join him but to be standing there, on his own if only briefly, the start, hopefully, of a solution, that was good.

"I think I'll put Four next," said Numberlina. "If I am to succeed, I need a number to stand four square with One. Four, stand next to One." Four took up a position alongside One. She was proud to be the second number to be called and nothing was going to move her. As one of the three numbers that had shown Piff how to make perfect right angles for all her carpentry work, Four felt particularly identified with Piff's cause.

"I'm not sure who should come next," said Numberlina. "But I do think Nine is the best candidate. He will round off the first prime number perfectly. We will have One at the start and Nine at the end, the first and last." Nine, as immaculate as ever, took his place beside Four. With his grey eyes, focused on the middle distance, his high cheekbones and firm chin, he was the perfect choice to complete the first prime number. He somehow conveyed perfectly the resolution of the numbers to fight and win for Piff.

"149," said Numberlina.

The Anathemath shifted uneasily.

"Now I will try for the second prime. There are only six numbers left, so it should be a little easier, but there are hundreds of permutations. I will start with Five. He is the middle number between One and Nine, so he seems the safest bet. Step forward, Five." Five stepped forward and took a position next to Nine but leaving a gap to indicate he was the start of the second prime. He felt it appropriate he should start the next prime number, given the high regard in which he was held by mankind. There was some rivalry between Nine and Five in terms of religious significance and Five could not help feeling gratified that he was the start of the second prime, while nine was merely the end of the first. And Five, like Four, was pleased to play his part. He also felt close to Piff because of the part he had played in solving the right-angle problem.

Numberlina paused, as though uncertain how to proceed. She surveyed the remaining numbers. Two, Three, Six, Seven and Eight were still available. "I think Eight should join Five," she said eventually. "I have chosen only one girl so far and I think Eight will give some balance to the second prime."

The word 'balance' elicited a snigger from Six. "Was that 'balance' or 'ballast'? she whispered to Three who, despite his embarrassment, had some difficulty in suppressing a smile.

"What did you say?" demanded Eight.

Numberlina intervened immediately. "This is no time for badinage. The fate of Piff and Numberland is at stake. Six, be quiet and wait your turn. Eight, stand next to Five."

Now the Anathemath had many faults – in fact he had almost every fault – but stupidity was not amongst them. He knew that, if Numberlina picked the next number correctly, she would have found two of the three primes needed to make a total of 999. She would still have to arrange the remaining three numbers correctly but what had seemed an insuperable problem at the start would now be easy to solve. After all, there would be only a few possible permutations and, in any case, she could simply subtract the two primes she had identified from 999 to find the third.

"I think Seven should end the second prime," said Numberlina. "Clearly I have to keep Six and Eight apart, and I don't want Seven to be with Six because I think they are a bad influence on each other." This was fair comment, given that the pretty Six couldn't resist goading the plump Eight about her figure and the roguish Seven always sided with and encouraged Six because he fancied her.

The Anathemath was not interested in Numberlina's reasoning, only in the conclusion.

"So I guess my second prime is 587," said Numberlina.

The Anathemath's eye narrowed. "I think there is very little guessing going on," he said. By now the green penumbra that surrounded him was seething.

"That leaves just Two, Three and Six, and the only prime number they can make is 263. So it seems I do have an answer," said a triumphant Numberlina. "149, 263, 587 are the three prime numbers, made up from the numbers 1 to 9. And, would you believe it, when you add them together, they total 999?"

I have not anywhere described what happens to the Anathemath when he is outwitted but I can tell you it is not a pretty sight or, to put no finer point upon it, it is not a fragrant smell. The centre of the green cloud dissolves, thickening the outer layers so that the whole becomes a seething thick green mass of noxious fumes.

"Everyone out," shouted Numberlina, holding her breath.

"We have much to do."

The numbers needed little encouragement. Of course they wanted to help Piff but, in any case, the smell within the outhouse was so foul that breathing it only briefly made you feel sick. Within a minute Numberlina and the numbers were out in the fresh air, hard at work amongst the vast throng of Numberlanders, explaining the figures that Piff had given them on the amount of tax Prince Baltigral took and pointing out how much better off they would be if they had a less greedy leader. Like a wave, hope and optimism spread across the Woodland Manor clearing and then out on all sides into the Numberland forest.

The vote was a clear-cut victory for Piff.

Prince Baltigral called on his personal guard to seize Piff but Tom O'Heneney explained to his erstwhile master that Piff now had the support of the people and, perhaps even more important, rather more money at her disposal than the prince. He explained that, if any one was to be arrested, it would not be Piff.

The celebrations went on for hours. Everyone, even those who had voted for the prince, wanted to congratulate Piff. But, eventually, Piff was able to find a quiet moment. She called for Numberlina. "I want to thank you and all the numbers from the bottom of my heart," said Piff.

"There is no need," said Numberlina. "You helped us in our struggle with the Anathemath and we helped you in your struggle with Baltigral."

"It's kind of you to say so, but I know how much I owe you. My family was poor; now we are rich. We had no power in the forest; now we can change the county. I am so much in your debt."

"Then tell the people of Numberland that the Numerati are ever ready to help, that the numbers are on their side and that, if anyone hopes to succeed, in life or in business, they should number the numbers amongst their most loyal and dependable friends."

49

A brave new day had dawned for Numberland. From that day on, under Piff's wise governance, those who showed the most creativity, initiative and, generally, had the most ability would receive the greatest respect and rewards. All those who worked hard would be well paid. Those who couldn't work would be well cared for. Those who were lazy would not be allowed to starve but they would be openly despised.

It was some days after the new dawn that Nine took Numberlina to one side and asked her the question that had been puzzling all the numbers. "How did you find the right combination of primes? We were all jigging about like mad things, but we couldn't find three primes to total 999."

Numberlina laughed: "I had some help. From Martha Viola, President of the Numerati High Council."

"But I thought the Anathemath had made them promise that they wouldn't give you the answer."

"Nor did they," said Numberlina. "Instead, Martha Viola told me a story."

Numberlina repeated the story, word for word.

Nine listened and, when Numberlina had finished, said, "I don't see how that helped. What has a sausage eating contest got to do with the Anathemath's challenge?"

"At first, that's exactly what I thought," said Numberlina, "and then it struck me. Twice in her story, Martha had said three words that made up a three digit number: 'When all the bets were in, most had bet for lower numbers but there was **one for nine**' and 'After much munching, there was a dead heat of several contestants. **Five ate seven**, a new Numberland sausage eating record'."

Still Nine didn't understand.

"It's simple, really," said Numberlina. "Martha said: 'one for nine', and 'five ate seven', or 149 and 587. All I had to do was add the two prime number together and subtract the total from 999 to find the third prime. We had the answer: 149, 263 and 587."

Nine laughed. "It seems you found the answer by solving a riddle. One in the eye for the Anathemath."

"Three riddles, actually," Numberlina grinned. "And that would be one in his only eye."

50

I suppose, dear reader, you would like to know what happened after Piff took charge of Numberland and I'd like to say that everyone lived happily ever after. But I can't because that's nonsense. No one lives for ever after, let alone always happily. Yes I know that's tough, but grow up.

I can say that Piff was a great success. Ship-building had its ups and down but the firewood and furniture business continued, generating regular income. Funnily enough, the real winner was Begingle, the alcoholic version of befangle juice. It was an unprecedented success in terms of making money, although its use, in excess, did cause quite a few social problems. In later years, long after the time of this story, it became known as gingle, and then later still, as gin.

Piff was a good and wise leader of her people. She kept close to her at all times the abacus Jack had given her, to remind herself how important maths was. And, if she ever had a problem she couldn't solve herself, which was rare, she had only to drop a tear on one of the beads and Numberlina would be with her in the twinkling of an eye.

Around her neck, Piff wore the gold medallion which Seven had presented to her on her 15th birthday on behalf of Numberlina and all the numbers. The perfectly balanced scales in the medallion reminded Piff every day to be fair in her dealings with everyone, with her workers, with her suppliers, with her customers and with all the people of Numberland. Some said the medallion was magic and somehow charmed Piff into being a just ruler. And Piff did nothing to discourage the idea. But, if the truth is told, Piff found that, in life and in business, if you are fair to others, they will be fair to you. And, if occasionally, someone lets you down, you can always kick them in the Goolies. In Numblish, the Goolies is a section of the forest where naughty children have to go to spend an hour or so reciting their 'times tables'.

While I think of it, in addition to gin, there is one other debt we owe the people of Numberland. When, many centuries later, the telephone was invented, the authorities chose 999 as the number to call for the police, an ambulance or the fire brigade. They wished to commemorate the Great Debate and the moment when the fate of Numberland hung in the balance and had to be saved by an excellent small being, with considerable aerodynamic and numerical skills, providing her own very special emergency service.

So, even after the boundary changes and the disappearance of Numberland in the latter part of the last century, there are still today reminders of that golden age when maths was so important it was guarded, preserved and revered by the exceedingly clever Martha Viola Fomes and the High Council of the Numerati.

And maths is still revered today, by anyone who really wants to succeed. The noxious Anathemath may attempt to tell you otherwise but I speak the truth. You can count on it.

MAIN CHARACTERS, IN ALPHABETICAL ORDER

Baltigral (Prince of Numberland) — Grab it all (anagram)

Jack (husband of Jill) — On loan from a nursery rhyme

Jill (second wife of Jack) — See above

Martha Viola Fomes (President, Numerati High Council) — I am a lover of maths (anagram)

Numberlina (member of the Numerati branch of the fairy family) — Distant relative of Thumberlina

Numbers (0 to 9) — Very much themselves

Redring (Chancellor of Numberland) — Grinder (anagram)

Ronald Albany Softcok (moneylender, aka Ronnie) — *Work it out for yourself* (anagram)

Piff — Herself (aka Stephanie)

Tom O'Heneny (Captain of the Guard) — On the money (anagram)

Winged Frodo (emblem of Ronnie's company) — *Work it out for yourself* (anagram)

NB: The Anathemath defies description

Most of Numberlina's working sheets have been lost but we have attempted to put together some of her workings. Although unlikely, some of these sheets may be of passing interest to one or two of our readers.

FIREWOOD BUSINESS

Four sacks (200 pieces) of wood a day/4 sausages a day
Rent 20p a day; Tax @ 50%

FAMILY COSTS	No/day	Price	SACKS Cost/day	Cst/Wk	£ YEAR
Sausages	4	5	20	140	7,280
Bread	2	3	6	42	2,184
Befangle Juice	2	3	6	42	2,184
Rent	1	20	20	140	7,280
Misc	2	20	40	280	14,560
Totals			**92**	**644**	**33,488**
BUSINESS					
Income					
Pieces of firewood	200				
Number of sacks	4	50	200	1,400	72,800
Costs					
Wood	0	0	0		
Sacks (0.1 per piece)	4	5	20	140	7,280
Employees	0	0	0	0	0
Horse & Cart	0	0	0	0	0
Net Income			180	1,260	65,520
Tax @ 50% of net income			90	630	32,760
BUSINESS PROFIT = / −			90	630	32,760
Family Costs			92	644	33,488
Family Net Income			-2	-14	-728

20 bundles (200 pieces) of wood a day @ 10p/4 sausages a day
Rent 20p a day; Tax @ 50%

FAMILY COSTS	No/day	Price	STRING Cost/day	Cst/Wk	£ YEAR
Sausages	4	5	20	140	7,280
Bread	2	3	6	42	2,184
Befangle Juice	2	3	6	42	2,184
Rent	1	20	20	140	7,280
Misc	2	20	40	280	14,560
Totals			92	644	33,488
BUSINESS					
Income					
Pieces of firewood	200				
Number of bundles	20	10	200	1,400	72,800
Costs					
Wood	0	0	0	0	0
String (0.02) per piece	20	0.02	0.40	3	146
Net Income			200	1,397	72,654
Tax @ 50% of net income			100	699	36,327
BUSINESS PROFIT = / –			**100**	**699**	**36,327**
			92	644	33,488
			8	55	2,839

20 bundles (200 pieces) of wood a day @ 12p/ 4 sausages a day
Rent 20p a day; Tax @ 50%

FAMILY COSTS	No/day	Price	STRING Cost/day	Cst/Wk	£ YEAR
Sausages	4	5	20	140	7,280
Bread	2	3	6	42	2,184
Befangle Juice	2	3	6	42	2,184
Rent	1	20	20	140	7,280
Misc	2	20	40	280	14,560
Totals			**92**	**644**	**33,488**
BUSINESS					
Income					
Pieces of firewood	200				
Number of bundles	20	12	240	1,680	87,360
Costs					
Wood	0	0	0	0	0
String (0.02) per piece	20	0.02	0.40	3	146
Net Income			240	1,677	87,214
Tax @ 50% of net income			120	839	43,607
BUSINESS PROFIT = / –			**120**	**839**	**43,607**
Family Costs			92	644	33,488
Family Net Income			28	195	10,119

25 bundles (250 pieces) of wood a day @ 10p/ 4 sausages a day
Rent 20p a day; Tax @ 50%

FAMILY COSTS	No/day	Price	STRING Cost/day	Cst/Wk	£ YEAR
Sausages	4	5	20	140	7,280
Bread	2	3	6	42	2,184
Befangle Juice	2	3	6	42	2,184
Rent	1	20	20	140	7,280
Misc	2	20	40	280	14,560
Totals			92	644	33,488
BUSINESS					
Income					
Pieces of firewood	250				
Number of bundles	25	10	250	1,750	91,000
Costs					
Wood	0	0	0	0	0
String (0.02) per piece	25	0.02	0.50	4	182
Net Income			250	1,747	90,818
Tax @ 50% of net income			125	873	45,409
BUSINESS PROFIT = / –			**125**	**873**	**45,409**
Family Costs			92	644	33,488
Family Net Income			33	229	11,921

25 bundles (250 pieces) of wood a day @ 12p/ 4 sausages a day
Rent 20p a day; Tax @ 50%

FAMILY COSTS	No/day	Price	STRING Cost/day	Cst/Wk	£ YEAR
Sausages	4	5	20	140	7,280
Bread	2	3	6	42	2,184
Befangle Juice	2	3	6	42	2,184
Rent	1	20	20	140	7,280
Misc	2	20	40	280	14,560
Totals			92	644	33,488
BUSINESS					
Income					
Pieces of firewood	250				
Number of bundles	25	12	300	2,100	109,200
Costs					
Wood	0	0	0	0	0
String (0.02) per piece	25	0.02	0.50	4	182
Net Income			300	2,097	109,018
Tax @ 50% of net income			150	1,048	54,509
BUSINESS PROFIT = / –			**150**	**1,048**	**54,509**
Family Costs			92	644	33,488
Family Net Income			58	404	21,021

25 bundles (250 pieces) of wood a day @ 12p/ 7 sausages a day
Rent 20p a day; Tax @ 50%

			STRING		
FAMILY COSTS	No/day	Price	Cost/day	Cst/Wk	£ YEAR
Sausages	7	5	35	245	12,740
Bread	2	3	6	42	2,184
Befangle Juice	2	3	6	42	2,184
Rent	1	20	20	140	7,280
Misc	2	20	40	280	14,560
Totals			107	749	38,948
BUSINESS					
Income					
Pieces of firewood	250				
Number of bundles	25	12	300	2,100	109,200
Costs					
Wood	0	0	0	0	0
String (0.02) per piece	25	0.02	0.50	4	182
Net Income			300	2,097	109,018
Tax @ 50% of net income			150	1,048	54,509
BUSINESS PROFIT = / –			150	1,048	54,509
Family Costs			107	749	38,948
Family Net Income			43	299	15,561

50 bundles (500 pieces) of wood a day @ 12p/ 7 sausages a day
Rent 20p a day; Tax @ 50%

			STRING		
FAMILY COSTS	No/day	Price	Cost/day	Cst/Wk	£ YEAR
Sausages	7	5	35	245	12,740
Bread	2	3	6	42	2,184
Befangle Juice	2	3	6	42	2,184
Rent	1	20	20	140	7,280
Misc	2	20	40	280	14,560
Totals			107	749	38,948
BUSINESS					
Income					
Pieces of firewood	500				
Number of bundles	50	12	600	4,200	218,400
Costs					
Wood	0	0	0	0	0
String (0.02) per piece	50	0.02	1.00	7	364
Net Income			599	4,193	218,036
Tax @ 50% of net income			300	2,097	109,018
BUSINESS PROFIT = / –			300	2,097	109,018
Family Costs			107	749	38,948
Family Net Income			193	1,348	70,070

250 bundles (2,500 pieces) of wood a day @ 12p/ 7 sausages a day
Rent 20p a day; Tax @ 50%

FAMILY COSTS	No/day	Price	EMPLOYEE Cost/day	Cst/Wk	£ YEAR
Sausages	7	5	35	245	12,740
Bread	2	3	6	42	2,184
Befangle Juice	2	3	6	42	2,184
Rent	1	20	20	140	7,280
Misc	3	20	60	420	21,840
Totals			127	889	46,228
BUSINESS					
Income					
Pieces of firewood	2,500				
Number of bundles	250	12	3,000	21,000	1,092,000
Costs					
Wood	0	0	0	0	0
String (0.02) per piece	250	0.02	5	35	1,820
Employees	10	100	1,000	7,000	364,000
Horse & Cart	10	40	400	2,800	145,600
Net Income			1,595	11,165	580,580
Tax @ 50% of net income			798	5,583	290,290
BUSINESS PROFIT = / –			**798**	**5,583**	**290,290**
Family Costs			127	889	46,228
Family Net Income			671	4,694	244,062

250 bundles (2,500 pieces) of wood a day @ 12p/ 7 sausages a day
Rent 40p a day; Tax @ 60%

FAMILY COSTS	No/day	Price	EMPLOYEE Cost/day	Cst/Wk	£ YEAR
Sausages	7	5	35	245	12,740
Bread	2	3	6	42	2,184
Befangle Juice	2	3	6	42	2,184
Rent	1	40	40	280	14,560
Misc	3	20	60	420	21,840
Totals			147	1,029	53,508
BUSINESS					
Income					
Pieces of firewood	2,500				
Number of bundles	250	12	3,000	21,000	1,092,000
Costs					
Wood	0	0	0	0	0
String (0.02) per piece	250	0.02	5	35	1,820
Employees	10	100	1,000	7,000	364,000
Horse & Cart	10	40	400	2,800	145,600
Net Income			1,595	11,165	580,580
Tax @ 60% of net income			957	6,699	348,348
BUSINESS PROFIT = / –			**638**	**4,466**	**232,232**
Family Costs			147	1,029	53,508
Family Net Income			491	3,437	178,724

Furniture Business

Years one, two and three							
PER MONTH SALES	Price	Number	Income	Yearly	Years	Totals
Beds, singles	1,500	40	60,000	720,000		
Beds, doubles	2,500	55	137,500	1,650,000		
Chairs, dining	200	200	40,000	480,000		
Chairs, armchairs	280	70	19,600	235,200		
Tables	2,500	40	100,000	1,200,000		
Cupboards	300	130	39,000	468,000		
Couches	200	30	6,000	72,000		
Miscellaneous	120	150	18,000	216,000		
TOTAL SALES		715	420,100	5,041,200		
LABOUR						
Carpenters	4,600	30	138,000	1,656,000		
Apprentice	900	40	36,000	432,000		
Tools	50	50	2,500	30,000		
Distribution %	5		21,005	252,060		
Sub Total			197,505	2,370,060		
OVERHEADS						
Management			4,200	50,400		
TOTAL COSTS			201,705	2,420,460	3	7,261,380
GROSS PROFIT			218,395	2,620,740	3	7,862,220
TAX @ 60%			131,037	1,572,444	3	4,717,332
NET PROFIT			87,358	1,048,296	3	3,144,888

Combines Net Profit, Year One and Year Three			
	Year One		Year Three
Furniture Profit	1,048,296	3	3,144,888
Firewood Profit	178,724	3	536,172
TOTAL	1,227,020	3	3,681,060
Numberlina 15%	184,053	3	552,159
Numberlina Gold	60.3	3	181
Net Profit	1,042,967	3	3,128,901

Ship-Building

SHIP-BUILDING		
YEAR ONE		
Customer	Gunnar	
No. of ship	1	
Cost	1,000,000	
Price	5,000,000	
Gross Profit	4,000,000	
Numberlina 15%	600,000	
Numberlina Gold	197	
Net Profit	**3,400,000**	
YEAR TWO		
Customer	Gunnar	
No. of ship	1	
Cost	2,000,000	
Price	7,000,000	
Gross Profit	5,000,000	
Numberlina 15%	750,000	1,350,000
Numberlina Gold	246	443
Net Profit	**4,250,000**	**7,650,000**
Customer	Aethelstan	
No. of ship	1	
Cost	2,000,000	
Price	8,000,000	
Gross Profit	6,000,000	
Numberlina 15%	900,000	2,250,000
Numberlina Gold	295	738
Net Profit	**5,100,000**	**12,750,000**

Compound Interest

One gold piece at 100% interest p.a.
Interest paid quarterly

	Total	Int. Rate %	Quarterly Interest
Period	1.00	100	0.250
1	1.25	100	0.313
2	1.56	100	0.391
3	1.95	100	0.488
4	**2.44**	100	0.610

Interest paid monthly

	Total	Int. Rate %	Monthly Interest
Period	1.00	100	0.083
1	1.08	100	0.090
2	1.17	100	0.098
3	1.27	100	0.106
4	1.38	100	0.115
5	1.49	100	0.124
6	1.62	100	0.135
7	1.75	100	0.146
8	1.90	100	0.158
9	2.06	100	0.171
10	2.23	100	0.186
11	2.41	100	0.201
12	**2.61**	100	0.218

Interest paid weekly

	Total	Int. Rate %	Weekly Interest
Period	1.00	100	0.02
1	1.02	100	0.02
2	1.04	100	0.02
3	1.06	100	0.02
4	1.08	100	0.02
5	1.10	100	0.02
6	1.12	100	0.02
7	1.14	100	0.02
8	1.16	100	0.02
9	1.19	100	0.02
10	1.21	100	0.02

11	1.23	100	0.02
12	1.26	100	0.02
13	1.28	100	0.02
14	1.31	100	0.03
15	1.33	100	0.03
16	1.36	100	0.03
17	1.38	100	0.03
18	1.41	100	0.03
19	1.44	100	0.03
20	1.46	100	0.03
21	1.49	100	0.03
22	1.52	100	0.03
23	1.55	100	0.03
24	1.58	100	0.03
25	1.61	100	0.03
26	1.64	100	0.03
27	1.67	100	0.03
28	1.70	100	0.03
29	1.74	100	0.03
30	1.77	100	0.03
31	1.80	100	0.03
32	1.84	100	0.04
33	1.87	100	0.04
34	1.91	100	0.04
35	1.95	100	0.04
36	1.99	100	0.04
37	2.02	100	0.04
38	2.06	100	0.04
39	2.10	100	0.04
40	2.14	100	0.04
41	2.18	100	0.04
42	2.23	100	0.04
43	2.27	100	0.04
44	2.31	100	0.04
45	2.36	100	0.05
46	2.40	100	0.05
47	2.45	100	0.05
48	2.50	100	0.05
49	2.54	100	0.05
50	2.59	100	0.05
51	2.64	100	0.05
52	**2.69**	100	0.05

www.ingramcontent.com/pod-product-compliance
Lightning Source LLC
Chambersburg PA
CBHW050537300426
44113CB00012B/2150